DATE DUE

DEC 29 1994	
APR 04 1995	
MAR 2 5 1997	
FEB 26 1998	
Mar 4, 1998	
NOV 05 1998	
JAN 29 1999	
MAR 16 2000	
APR 26 2002	

Max Weber's Sociology of Intellectuals

Max Weber's Sociology of Intellectuals

Ahmad Sadri

With a Foreword by
Arthur J. Vidich

New York   Oxford
OXFORD UNIVERSITY PRESS
1992

Oxford University Press

Oxford   New York   Toronto
Delhi   Bombay   Calcutta   Madras   Karachi
Kuala Lumpur   Singapore   Hong Kong   Tokyo
Nairobi   Dar es Salaam   Cape Town
Melbourne   Auckland

and associated companies in
Berlin   Ibadan

Library of Congress Cataloging-in-Publication Data
Sadri, Ahmad.
Max Weber's sociology of intellectuals / Ahmad Sadri ;
with a foreword by Arthur J. Vidich.
p. cm.   Includes bibliographical references.
ISBN 0-19-506556-5
1. Intellectuals. 2. Weber, Max, 1864–1920. I. Title.
HM213.S22   1992   305.5'52—dc20   92-4395

1 3 5 7 9 8 6 4 2

Printed in the United States of America
on acid-free paper

For my mother
Vadjihah Moulaie

Foreword

Arthur J. Vidich

Ahmad Sadri begins with the observation that neither intellectuals nor anti-intellectuals have been able to define exactly what an intellectual is, or to distinguish the functions of an intelligentsia from those of intellectuals. In his brief but closely argued study, Sadri provides a new way of looking at the intellectuals and intelligentsia and an answer to questions about their roles and functions in society. Out of a vast range of scholarly speculation, he has brought order to a subject that up to now has defied the best efforts of social theorists.

Sadri asserts that attempts by other scholars to explain the roles and functions of intellectuals and intelligentsia remain embedded in their commitments to various ideologies. For example, Karl Marx conceives of the intellectual as an alienated member of the upper classes who can transcend the limits of his or her class experience only at the moment of impending revolution. This action enabled the intellectual to at once arrive at the truth about society and to become a leader of the proletariat. Sadri sees this position as a special case of the revolutionary intellectual. Karl Mannheim's inversion of Marx's view defines the intellectual as someone who is free from the blindness of class-bound or official ideology; thereby, he or she is able to see the truth and to transform society from the perspective of that truth. For Sadri, however, this does not constitute a sociological explanation, but rather the limiting case of intellectual transcendence; one that leads to the creation of new world images.

In a masterfully synthetic review of most of the literature on intellectuals, Sadri locates and delimits the perspectives on intellectuals of such major European authors as V. I. Lenin, Rosa Luxemburg, Georg Lukacs, Joseph Schumpeter, Hannah Arendt, Ernst Bloch, Antonio Gramsci, George Orwell, Leszek Kolakowski, and George Konrad and Ivan Szelenyi. He also examines the ideas about intellectuals to be found in such American authors as Lester Ward, Willaim Graham Sumner, Talcott Parsons, Alvin Gouldner, and Russel Jacoby. Noting that the term *intelligentsia* originated in Russia, where it referred to the educated middle and upper classes whose concern was with social, economic, and political philosophy and with the arts, literature, and politics, Sadri goes on to present a comprehensive paradigm that isolates those characteristics that distinguish intellectuals from an intelligentsia. This paradigm appears in Chapter 4 and provides a starting point as well as a grounding for any future scholarly work on the subject of an intelligentsia or on intellectuals.

Sadri's own starting point is Max Weber's perspective on intellectuals as it can be drawn out of the latter's sociology of Indian, Chinese, Hebrew, and Western religions and civilizations. In his studies of world religions, Weber asked such questions as: What is the relation of ideas to social reality? What is the societal status of the carriers of ideas? Do such carriers create ideas independently or reflect class or other stratum-bound traditions? Do they lead progressive movements in society or do they observe and follow? What are the rational or irrational consequences that flow from a commitment to a given set of ideas or values? Keeping in mind Weber's questions, Sadri deconstructs Weber's analyses of religion in order to focus attention on those strata who are significant carriers of a civilization's religious and secular values. Such carriers have included the emissary and exemplary prophets of Judaism, the priestly class of Brahmins, the Confucian literati, and the itinerant Christian missionaries. But, as Weber put it, these carriers have included apparently secularized representatives:

> If one wishes to characterize succinctly, in a formula so to speak, the types of representatives of the various strata that were the primary

carriers or propagators of the so-called world religions, they would be the following: In Confucianism, the world-organizing bureaucrat; in Hinduism, the world ordering magician; in Buddhism, the medicant monk wandering through the world; in Judaism, the wandering trader; and in Christianity, the itinerant journeyman.

Guided by the categories developed by Weber in his studies of world religions, Sadri notes that Weber based his sociology of intellectuals on a "delicate balance between two theoretical assumptions":

> First he postulated the "relative autonomy" of the sphere of ideas from socioeconomic forces. Second, Weber proceeded with a theory of historical causation that we have dubbed "reverse determination," whereby the interest is shifted from the origin to the popularization of a religion according to the ideal and material interests of various strata and classes. The relative significance of these assumptions varies according to the level of analysis and the empirical characteristics of a particular form of intellectuality under investigation.

Citing one example of this delicate balance, Sadri notes how problems abound in studying the history of ideas and their carriers in the absence of the aforementioned twin assumptions. To make this point, he cites a very common phenomenon:

> The producers of ideas which are inimical to the ideologies of the intellectual class, or the class which patronizes them, are also intellectuals.

It is to overcome such problems that Sadri opens and expands Weber's sociology of intellectuals. Similarly, following Weber, he notes that the disenchantment of the world makes a religious flight from mundanity difficult for secular intellectuals. Yet these intellectuals must confront the irrationality of a world that does not allow them to escape from it. Intellectual responses to this dilemma, as, for example, it is posed by post-Protestant industrialism and its discontents, can lead to unexpected intellectual reactions. Among these is the reification of instrumental reason in the social sciences. These and other observations make it necessary for Sadri to include in his paradigm a variety of social types—scientists, social critics, this-worldly bureaucrats, researchers, abstract theorists—that might not otherwise be identified as intellectuals.

To give coherence to this congeries of types, Sadri classifies them according, on the one hand, to the commitment they make either to the discovery of truth or to a mission they have for the people—i.e., their social engagement—and, on the other, to their commitment to either theoretical or practical reason. The fourfold table derived from these categories ingeniously provides a way to differentiate such diverse types as scientists, scholars, theorists, theologians, priests, bureaucrats, media specialists, reformers, lawyers, and revolutionaries by their attitude and social function. It also evokes a set of ideal types that might be used by a researcher engaged in further empirical study of either intellectuals or an intelligentsia.

Sadri is well aware that the creation of ideal types in itself does not substitute for empirical research; rather such types are heuristic devices enabling the researcher to conceptualize, analyze, and resolve a particular problem. Although the pure resolution of conceptual ambiguities is not the essential task of a social science, he understands that such resolutions are necessary when ambiguity interferes with empirical investigations.

The conceptual clarification supplied by Sadri would not have been possible had he not been a close reader of Weber's methodological writings. In his first chapter, "Max Weber's Methodology," Sadri explains and justifies the relevance of Weber's methodology to his own reconstruction of Weber's sociology of intellectuals. At issue here is the question of how it is possible to compare and contrast, from the perspective and with the languages of Western civilization, other, nonoccidental world civilizations. In the past, such comparisons have led to accusations of Western epistemological and cultural imperialism and to charges of an occidental desire to monopolize the creation of world images. Sadri explains his resolution of this problem:

> The apparent "generalizations" on the basis of which our model is based are not inductively constructed; concepts such as intellectuals, intelligentsia, men of knowledge are heuristic devices. For one thing, these concepts do not claim to represent ontologically significant and universal phenomena. Rather they bear the imprint of particular

historical and geocultural "value relevant interests" of Western civilization.

Yet while recognizing that Weber's and his own concepts are temporally and geoculturally grounded, Sadri does not give up the task of comparing and contrasting different civilizations. To grasp Sadri's reason for beginning his study with an examination of Weber's methodology, one must understand the logical structure of this book, a study which begins and ends in Chapter 4 on the theme of the relationship between the codification of theory and a heuristic approach to theory. The reader will find Sadri's rationale for the defense of heuristic theory both provocative and convincing.

By including five appendices in his study, Sadri has revived the art of the appendix as a device for clarifying tangential but critical substantive and theoretical issues. In Appendix C he is led to correct Weber's interpretation of Islam as a warrior religion and to comment on Bryan S. Turner's *Weber and Islam*, noting that "Islam's radical monotheism (singularity of the divine in principle) would thwart the warrior's characteristic penchant for polytheism, monolatry or henotheism." In this appendix, Sadri provides a new starting point for a reassessment and reinterpretation of Islamic intellectualism. Appendix D, "Ideologies and Counterideologies of Intellectuals in Occidental East and West," shows the similarities in ideological responses of intellectuals in Eastern and Western Europe (including the United States), revealing that "similar ideological needs can generate similar ideologies." Here Sadri compares two ideologues, Lester Ward and Lenin, with two counterideologues, William G. Sumner and Rosa Luxemburg. Lenin and Ward opposed the Spencerian gospel of evolution, arguing like Comte that a scientific politics would replace it and its irrationalities. For Ward a stratum of sociocrats would "work for all mankind and for all time, and all they ask is that all mankind shall forever benefit by their work. . . . they only ask an opportunity to apply scientific principles to great things." Lenin calls his elite "a dozen trained and talented" persons and assigns to them the task of shaping the consciousness of the proletariat whom they would also represent. Sadri's capacity to see such elective affinities in the thought processes of Ward and Lenin, let alone his possession of the imagination to venture forth in such an enterprise, reveals his capacity for finding intercultural common elements in culturally disparate ideologies.

Treating Sumner and Luxemburg as counterideologues, one in the tradition of sociology and the other in socialism, Sadri points to the affinities in intellectual tactics that each uses. Both uphold the value of evolution as opposed to revolutionary intervention to accomplish social change:

> the only possible good must come from evolution not revolution. (Sumner)

> Stop the natural pulsation of a living organism and you weaken it, and you diminish its resistance and combatative spirit. (Luxemburg)

Sumner and Luxemburg hold to a belief in the automaticity of social evolution and oppose and criticize the intervention of intellectuals in the hope of controlling or directing its trajectory. The reader of this comparison of Sumner and Luxemburg cannot help but be impressed by Sadri's ability to enter into the intellectual world of the other and to see therein commonalities in thought patterns that cut across national boundaries and civilizations.

The author of this book is himself a product of two civilizations. Formed by an education in classical Persian scholarship, Sadri continued his studies in classical and contemporary social theory at the Graduate Faculty of the New School for Social Research in the United States. His willingness to expose himself to contrasting intellectual world views facilitates the originality of his approach to his subject—who before him had thought of comparing Lenin and Ward to Sumner and Luxemburg?—and testifies to his remarkable insight into the thought-ways and world images of a diverse company of the modern world's intellectuals. His reconstruction of a sociology of intellectuals from Weber's sociology of religion is itself a major contribution to Weberian scholarship. His formulation of a heuristic general theory of intellectuals and intelligentsia is independently significant, a major contribution to contemporary social thought.

Contents

Max Weber's Sociology of Intellectuals

1

Methodology of Social Sciences

Methodology Again

It is neither the conventional etiquette of Weberian scholarship nor a peculiar logical predilection that prompts us to begin a book about intellectuals with a chapter on methodology. To console those with a distaste for the formal and the abstract, let us recall that Weber himself regarded the obsessive methodological discussions of his time with a sense of detachment and even irony. Why then did he defer pursuing his main interest in the grand, substantive sociological and historical questions, to dedicate a few years of his life to methodological reflections, ultimately contributing to what he had dubbed the "methodological pestilence"? There are good reasons to believe that the prime motive of Max Weber to work on methodology was to provide a viable answer to the *Methodenstreit*, the protracted controversy between the legacy of Enlightenment as represented in the theoretically abstract arguments of the Austrian school of economics on the one side, and the Romantic individualism and historicism of the German historical school on the other.[1] Without rejecting the prior suggestion, I would like to advance the thesis that the purpose of Weber's methodological reflections was to mend a problem that was intrinsic to his own universe of discourse. Weber's methodology represents an immanent attempt to bridge the gap that existed between his own individualistic epistemological and methodological premises, on one hand, and the kind of intellectual apparatus he needed for the pursuit of his interest in substantive civilizational and historical analyses, on the other. It is not reasonable to assume that Weber

3

was oblivious to this tension, nor to regard his methodology as a whimsical exercise in solving a conceptual puzzle.

If the following discussion has any validity, then it might be stated that Weber succeeded in closing the tremendous cleavage that threatened the inner consistency of his intellectual cosmos. Thus Weber could remain true to his methodological axioms throughout his substantive work.

The main object of this chapter is to underscore the inner consistency of Weber's work. Weber's methodology had a remedial character. He did not intend to provide guidelines for the conduct of research either for himself or for others.[2] Even the most celebrated outcome of Weber's methodology, the ideal typical analysis, is admittedly not an invention but a rediscovery. Weber believed modern historiography (Weber, *Objectivity*, p. 92) as well as abstract theoretical expositions in social sciences (Weber, *Objectivity*, pp. 88–103) to be suffused with ideal types. He merely suggested that these constructs be deployed more consciously. In this chapter we also hope to highlight the relevance of Weber's methodology to our reconstruction of his sociology of intellectuals. Throughout this book we will deal with questions such as the role of intellectuals in history, the interplay of ideas and interests, and the role of the carriers of ideas in the development of ideologies that serve various interests. The final chapter aspires to function as a taxonomical guide to projects in a "Weberian sociology of intellectuals." By this we mean not only the sum total of Weber's observations on sociology of intellectuals, which are organized throughout the book, but also a set of ideal types and epistemological and methodological assumptions about the identity and functions of intellectuals. Such general concepts cannot be proposed without first establishing the metatheoretical groundwork that will be suggested in the present chapter. This chapter consists of three sections.

In the first section we will try to demonstrate how Weber's methodology both embraced and transcended his epistemological axioms. Had these assumptions not been modified and mediated by his methodology, they would have created an unfit framework for his substantive studies. The aims of this section are therefore to establish that Weber's sociology of intellectuals is compatible with and deeply rooted in his epistemological and methodological assumptions. Of course, understanding Weber's substantive studies does not presuppose an explication of his theory of concept formation. Yet, Weber engaged in such explorations in order to solve the problems that arose in the course of his empirical research. Since such problems usually result from the uncritical introduction of erroneous metatheoretical assumptions, Weber's attempts usually aim at weeding out such assumptions rather than establishing methodology for the social sciences. Regarding the magnitude of theoretical and empirical problems involved in the sociology of intellectuals, it would be an error to start such a venture without taking precautions against the intrusion of metatheoretical errors.

The second section of this chapter focuses on Weber's conception of historical causality and its interdependence with the specific interests of the historian. Understanding Weber's solution of this problem is crucial for all historical sciences in general and for the sociology of intellectuals in particular. For instance, Weber's assertion that intellectuals "influence" the trajectory of history, that they have been, in certain instances, the carriers of ideas, and that they have determined the developmental course of civilizations can easily be misconstrued if it is not understood within the context of his theory of historical causation.

A sociology of intellectuals would be incomplete if it failed to clarify its stance toward various theories of social change with regard to the role they assign to the intellectuals in sociohistorical developments. The closing section of the first chapter is dedicated to a reexamination of the theories of social change in relation to Weber's concept of "social selection." Weber, however, shrank from highlighting the significance of his theory of "social selection," because he believed that methodological arguments cannot guide substantive research. For him such arguments only served purposes of self-clarification. Indeed, self-clarification had become all the more necessary for Weber and his readers because they moved in an intellectual atmosphere that was ever so heavily scented by the philosophies of history propounded in the two preceding centuries.

Escape from Methodological Nominalism

Weber's interpretive sociology had to overcome the formidable obstacle of constructing the apparatus of a science fit to study the grand social and historical problems without using the hypostatized and collectivistic notions that pervaded the social sciences of his time. He needed also to advance beyond an abstract negation of collectivism and to rehabilitate some of its concepts to establish a conceptual mooring for a noncollectivist science of society and history. In 1920, a few months before his death, Weber wrote:

> If I have become a sociologist it is mainly in order to exorcise the specter of collective conceptions which will linger among us. In other words, sociology itself can only proceed from the actions of one or more separate individuals and must, therefore, adopt strictly individualistic methods.[3]

This statement and the ones that follow,[4] betray an extreme brand of methodological individualism. This could have bred a skeptical kind of sociological nominalism if not psychological reductionism. But Weber chose neither path. He even did not tread the "phenomenological," social interactionist, and generally speaking "micro-sociological" route, which he certainly paved for others to explore. Weber's sociological interests demanded the larger domain of social and intercivilizational studies. This left him with a hiatus within his universe of discourse. Weber developed his "interpretive sociology" so as to cross this gap in three major strides: (1) to expel the "actual existing meaning" from the domain of sociology, (2) to substitute the concept of probability of social action for the notion of reciprocity in social relationships, and finally, (3) to establish the ideal typical analysis as the principal vehicle of interpretive sociology, and of historical sciences.[5]

Step One: Doing Away with "Actual Existing Meaning"

At the outset of his best known methodological work,[6] Max Weber made it clear that sociology, as he defined it, is concerned with the interpretive understanding of social action. He spoke of action, of course, when the acting individual attaches meaning to his "behavior." But he was quick to add:

> "Meaning" may be of two kinds. The term may refer first to the actual existing meaning in the given concrete case of a particular

actor, or to the average or approximate meaning attributable to a given plurality of actors; or secondly to the theoretically conceived *pure type* of subjective meaning attributed to the hypothetical actor or actors in a given type of action. (Weber, *Economy I*, p. 4)

It is of cardinal importance for a correct understanding of Weber's "interpretive sociology" to bear in mind that it scarcely deals with "actual existing meaning."[7] Weber was especially averse to making the first subcategory of actual existing meaning (that possessed by a given concrete actor) the subject matter of sociology. For starters, the difficulties concerning the attainment and verification of the actual existing meaning are insurmountable. Weber offered no answer to this polemical question of the positivists: How can we get to the back of the mind of a particular actor? He agreed that there is no guarantee that the best reproduction of the meaning that a particular actor ascribes to his or her behavior, in the mind of the most sympathetic of all observers, would correspond to the actual meaning in the mind of the actor in question (Weber, *Knies*, pp. 179, 180). Besides, the intuitive inner understanding of the totality of the feelings of a particular individual produces, at best, a vague and unverifiable image that can hardly be called "knowledge," let alone "scientific knowledge."[8] By dismissing actual existing meaning from the realm of sociological interest Weber saves himself the trouble of "verifying" these elusive meanings.[9]

We can trace Weber's lack of interest in actual existing meaning to roots other than the mere difficulties of attainment and verification. Even if an observer could properly obtain and verify the concrete subjectivity of a social actor, this knowledge could not be relied upon by a Weberian social scientist as anything but raw data. In other words, the ultimate criterion for the validity of the observer's interpretations is not its agreement with the so-called native's account. This, of course, goes against the conventional picture of Weber as the father of *Verstehen* sociology, for which he has been alternatively admired (Ritzer, 1975, p. 86) and censured (Strauss, 1953, p. 55). No. Weber did not trust the "understanding" of the social actor as the ultimate criterion of validity for interpretive sociology:

The "conscious motives" may well, even to the actor himself, conceal the various "motives" and "repressions" which constitute the real driving force of his action. Thus in such cases even subjectively honest self-analysis has only a relative value. Then it is the task of the sociologist to be aware of this motivational situation and to describe and analyze it, even though it has not actually been concretely part of the conscious intention of the actor; possibly not all, at least not fully. (Weber, *Economy I*, pp. 9, 10)

Here Weber is raising the problem of "false consciousness"—which until recently was a popular motif in the Marxist literature—to undermine the significance of the actual existent meaning for the purposes of scientific analysis. It is not only the possibility of "false consciousness" but also the prevalence of "semiconsciousness" that dissuaded Weber from studying the intentionality of the concrete individual. "Semiconscious" behavior comprises all the marginal cases of meaningful action such as affectual, imitative, habitual, or traditional action (Weber, *Economy I*, pp. 4–25). Besides, social actors often act under the influence of a plurality of impulses, which makes it difficult to arrive at an approximate estimate of the relative strength of their conflicting motives (Weber, *Economy I*, p. 10). Finally, it must be mentioned that a search for the actual existing meaning does not help the cause of the sciences of empirical reality (*Wirklichkeitswissenschaft*), which is to overcome the multiplicity of empirical reality. It is the task of sociology to first view all the meaningful phenomena that are within its realm and then to find a way of scientifically reducing the immensity of the empirical data. (Weber suggests constructing a model against which the relevant facts can be measured.) To revert to the study of the actual existing meaning blurs the focus of sociology and defeats the purpose of the selective process of science.[10]

The average or approximate meaning attributable to a given plurality of actors is the second variety of actual existing meaning.[11] Does this constitute the subject matter of interpretive sociology? Only in a marginal sense, because:

average types, can be formulated with a relative degree of precision only where they are concerned with differences of degree in respect to action which remains qualitatively the same. Such cases do occur, but in the majority of cases of action important to history or sociology the motives which determine it are qualitatively heterogeneous.

Then it is quite impossible to speak of an "average" in the true sense.
(Weber, *Economy I*, pp. 20–21)

Thus, the ideal types used in economics and sociology should not
be confused with average types, nor should they be mistaken for the
laws of behavior pertaining to the uniformities. The quasi-general
aspects of social and economic ideal types do not represent concrete
meanings in the minds of actual individuals. They are the results of
"dogmatically ascribed" maxims and priorities to the "hypothetical" social actors. This means that the use of average types is
practically limited to the sociological mass phenomena (Weber,
Economy I, p. 9). This argument also provides a partial vindication
for the quantitative methods of empirical sociology. Weber would
agree that the hypotheses of these studies must be "verified"
through empirical research because their object is a variant of
actual existing meaning. To enlarge on this point would necessitate
an elaboration of Weber's response to such trends as positivism,
which contributed to the rise of empirical sociology. The way in
which he moved to meet this challenge is discussed in Appendix A.

Step Two: From Interactive Reciprocity to Probabilistic Action

Weber professed to have done his best to "exorcise the specter of
collective concepts" from the realm of sociology.[12] If, while doing
so, he also managed to avoid the pitfall of taking the elusive
facticity of the concrete intersubjectivity of particular social actors
as the locus of interpretive sociology, it was partly because of his
peculiar interpretation of the concepts of "reciprocity" and "probability." This crucial theoretical move leading to the development of
the theory of ideal types enabled Weber to redefine, analytically
work out, and eventually rehabilitate and use some of those hypostatized "collective concepts" that once offended his epistemological
taste so much.

Although Weber established the necessity of the mutual intersubjective orientation as the essential component of "social action," he
radically undermined it as a constitutive element of "social relationships." Meaningful action can be nonsocial; it becomes social only
when it is oriented toward the meaningful action of others. Never-

theless, symmetry and reciprocity of the actual subjective orientation is not the locus of "social relationships":

> The subjective meaning need not necessarily be the same for all the
> parties who are mutually oriented in a given social relationship; there
> need not in this sense be "reciprocity." "Friendship," "love,"
> "loyalty," "fidelity to contracts," "patriotism," on one side, may well
> be faced with an entirely different attitude on the other. In such cases
> the parties associate different meanings with their actions, and the
> social relationship is insofar objectively "asymmetrical" from the
> points of view of the two parties. (Weber, *Economy I*, p. 27)

"Social relationship" is not based on intersubjective meetings of
the minds but (especially for the observer) on the "probability that
there will be a meaningful course of action." Note how Weber, using
his interpretation of the concepts of probability and reciprocity,
provides a new basis for the legitimate use of the collective concepts.

> That a "friendship" or a "state" exists or has existed means this and
> only this: that we, the observers, judge that there is or has been a
> probability that on the basis of certain kinds of known subjective
> attitudes of certain individuals there will result in the average sense a
> certain specific type of action. (Weber, *Economy I*, p. 28)

Thus, the actual psychic inner states of the participants in social
relationships, even when they are contradictory, become "immate-
rial" as long as "in effect the probability of that orientation to the
agreement actually exists to a sociologically relevant degree"
(Weber, *Logos*, p. 160). This makes it possible to treat certain
complexes of social action "as if" a uniform orientation toward a
given order exists among the participants. The market is an ideal
typical complex of actions of this kind and exhibits the characteristics introduced before (Weber, *Logos*, p. 167).

When a worker accepts "certain characteristically shaped metal
disks or slips of paper" as remunerations for his labor, he does so
knowing that an unspecified and totally anonymous multitude of
persons known as "others" are willing to exchange certain needed
goods for his "money." He also reckons that if someone should try

to deprive him of his earned goods "there is a certain possibility that people with spiked helmets would respond to his call and help him get them back" (Weber, *Stammler*, p. 101). Most sociological ideal types aim at characterizing these intersubjectively accessible expectations rather than delving into the psychic inner states of the social actors. Weber's special treatment of the concepts of reciprocity and probability not only moves us farther away from the type of interpretive knowledge of the actual existing meaning at the level of the concrete individual; it also sets the stage for Weber's final statement on the subject of interpretive sociology as he sees it: the ideal typical analysis.

Step Three: Interpretive Sociology Based on Ideal Types

Now it is reasonably clear that the kind of meaning interpretive sociology is mainly interested in is "the theoretically conceived *pure type* of subjective meaning attributed to the hypothetical actor or actors" (Weber, *Economy I*, p. 4). In what remains of this section we will state four of the main characteristics of ideal types, stressing the significance of each for the sociology of intellectuals. Let us start by elucidating the most obvious feature of ideal typical analysis:

1. *Ideal types are purely instrumental for sociology and social sciences. As such they are at once indispensable and insufficient.* There are different kinds of ideal types,[13] but they all have one thing in common: they are of "practical" value for sociological and historical analysis (Weber, *Meaning*, p. 42). They are temporary harbors in the sea of empirical facts, not the final destination (Weber, *Objectivity*, p. 104). To treat ideal types as anything more than "instrumental" would culminate in "reification" of ideal types.[14]

Let us see how Weber recommended the use of the "rationalistic" ideal types of action in sociology. Reality is "messy," it is not rational. In any given course of action, errors in thought or computation can be as consequential for the final outcome of the action as correct thinking and calculation. Nevertheless, Weber suggests the construction of a rational, thoroughly "errorless" trajectory for action. Among the varieties of collective action, war presents a notoriously jumbled combination of rational calculations and irrational outcomes. Nevertheless Weber suggests:

> To understand how a war is conducted, it is necessary to imagine an ideal commander-in-chief for each side—even though not explicitly or in detailed form. Each of these commanders must know the total fighting resources of each side and all the possibilities arising therefrom of attaining the concretely unambiguous goal, namely, the destruction of the enemy's military power. On the basis of this knowledge, they must act entirely without error and in a logically "perfect" way. For only then can the consequences of the fact that the real commanders neither had the knowledge nor were they free from error, and that they were not purely rational thinking machines, be unambiguously established. (Weber, *Meaning*, p. 42)

It is evident that the "rationalistic" character of this analysis is purely heuristic; it does not imply the predominance of the rational elements in human thought, much less a valuation of rationalism. The only drawback of these "rationalistic" ideal types is their "teleological" nature. By assuming a rational end for action, this method cannot help but imply a functionalist attitude in sociology: every action must be linked to a prefigured goal regardless of whether it is achieved or not. Weber frankly admits this implication and states (as many sociologists have also done) that the functional approach could even be useful as a "preliminary step" in sociological investigations (Weber, *Economy I*, p. 16). In criticizing Knies's arguments, Weber is even more candid about the "heuristic" value of this kind of ideal type. Here Weber implies that the assumption of rationality is a cryptographic device. We need to assume the coherence of the message if we are to make sense of it.

> "Interpretation" in our sense would be called for only in cases of the following description. Although the "meaning" of an expression is *not* immediately "understood," and it is not possible to reach a practical "understanding" concerning its meaning with its author, nevertheless an "understanding" of its meaning is of unconditional practical necessity. Consider an example which remains within the domain of "everyday" real life. An officer leading a patrol receives a written military command which is ambiguously drawn up. It is necessary for him to "interpret" the "purpose" of the order—that is to say, to consider the *motives* responsible for the order—in order to act on it. (Weber, *Knies*, p. 154)

Ideal types of social action must have a rational core even though action itself may lack rational structure. Thus an interrelated set of statistical correlations about a social phenomenon in isolation from an ideal typical meaning construction does not qualify as "interpretive sociology." At the same time, a perfectly rational ideal type of action is also useless if some kind of proof for the probable occurrence of the meaningful action is not provided (Weber, *Economy I*, p. 12). This mutual interdependence of ideal types and empirical data does not imply that the validity of ideal type must be "verified" by the empirical data. Weber's phraseology for this interdependence is: determining the "causal adequacy" of the "meaningfully adequate" course of action.

> Statistical uniformities constitute understandable types of action, and thus constitute sociological generalizations, only when they can be regarded as manifestations of the understandable subjective meaning of a course of social action. Conversely, formulations of a rational course of subjectively understandable action constitute sociological types of empirical process only when they can be empirically observed with a significant degree of approximation. (Weber, *Economy I*, p. 12)

The intuitive "self-evidence" of any subjectively adequate ideal type is deceptive. Weber warns against confusing this image of action with the empirical certainty that the sociologist must achieve[15] (Weber, *Knies*, p. 180; *Meaning*, p. 42). We must be aware that without a rigorous methodological screening of the sociological concepts, the ideal types of rational action might come innocently to present themselves as the "laws of human action," while the historical ideal types might appear as "logical trends of history." Logically speaking, ideal types are but stylized images obtained through abstractions and generalizations, eliminations and exaggerations. Their only aim is to substitute the "infinite multiplicity of successively and co-existently emerging and disappearing events" (Weber, *Objectivity*, p. 72). These ideal types, when compared with the infinite richness of empirical data, are relatively empty of concrete content (Weber, *Economy I*, p. 20). Weber admits that even historical ideal types are in this sense "unhistorical" (Weber, *Social*, p. 294).

Weber further underscored the instrumental nature of the sociological ideal types by pointing out that they are neither logical definitions nor general statements about a class of facts; they are purely fictitious "hypotheses" that are used to make a "scientific" understanding of the infinitely rich "empirical reality" humanly possible. With numerous examples, Weber illustrated that in those cases where ideal typical constructions seem to influence the concrete course of action, the process is always mediated by actual social actors. In the case of direct influence of the legal order on conduct, for instance, it is not the "law" but "the empirically *ascertainable maxim* of the concrete conduct of human beings" (Weber, *Stammler*, p. 130) that influence the action of others. People orient their behavior according to the probabilities that certain individuals (say judges) would take the legal ideas as the maxims of their action. Therefore, the legal order in fact exists as a set of maxims (Weber, *Stammler*, p, 129): "It is a norm which can be conceived as having 'axiological validity.' Therefore, it is quite obviously not a form of being or existence, but rather a standard of value by reference to which empirical existence can be evaluated." It is in this sense that Weber attributes causal significance to rationality.

Underestimating Weber's clarity of vision regarding the difference of ideal types of generalized action and those referring to the historical course of action, Talcott Parsons maintained that Weber had confused two different kinds of ideal types and thus attributed historical reality to the ideal typical construction of rationalization (Parsons, 1964). This is unlikely. Weber was well aware of the fictitious nature of the ideal type of rationality. However, he also believed that an ideal type, if mediated by human agents (in which case it becomes a "maxim" for the concrete actors), is capable of influencing the actual course of action and, consequently, of becoming a force in history.

Intellectuals, as we will see in the forthcoming chapter, often acted as such mediators; they are the bearers of different levels and modes of rationality. The rationalization of the sphere of ideas occurs through intellectuals who have a stake in constructing ever more consistent images of the world. This general statement can be used as a guide to study the substantively diverse contents of various civilizations and the role intellectuals have played in creating and developing the main thrust of ideas of that particular culture. It is always instructive to remember that theoretical (or practical for that matter) rationalization is not an independent force but a maxim in the minds of a group of individuals. Ideal types

> enable us to see if, in particular traits or in their total character, the phenomena approximate one of our constructions: to determine the degree of approximation of the historical phenomenon to the theoretically constructed type. To this extent, the construction is merely a technical aid which facilitates a more lucid arrangement and terminology. Yet, under certain conditions, a construction might mean more. For the rationality, in the sense of logical or teleological "consistency," of an intellectual-theoretical or practical-ethical attitude has and always has had power over man, however limited and unstable this power is and always has been in the face of other forces of historical life. Religious interpretations of the world and ethics of religions created by intellectuals and meant to be rational have been strongly exposed to the imperative of consistency. (Weber, *Rejections*, p. 324)

This is the reason behind Weber's suggestion that "the truth value of ideas is the guiding value in writing of intellectual history." The ideal types are not by themselves concrete forces in history, they do not constitute a mode of being (Weber, *Objectivity*, p. 93), yet their assumption, like that of the numerical order, helps one to sort out and comprehend the existing world. When they are taken seriously as maxims of action by certain strata (e.g., intellectuals), they become "real." Our last chapter contains a series of interrelated ideal types of intellectuals. These are admittedly only empty vessels that may or may not be filled in a given case of civilizational analysis. They become real in so far as the agents (intellectuals or intelligentsia) embody them. But it must also be emphasized that this manner of classification is itself as much a logical conjecture as it is a culturally specific one. It is not part of reality but rather of logic and culture. To better understand this we need to explain our second statement in relation to ideal types. Here we modify the already emphasized fictitiousness of the ideal types and encourage reflection on the nature of their falseness.

2. *Ideal types stylize the concrete reality, yet their distortions are by no means arbitrary; their falseness is a reflection of the observer's rootedness in time and space, and not the product of an artistic falsification.* This distortion is not only logically necessary.

It is also indispensable from the point of view of the "sociology of knowledge." It is our historical interests that determine the cultural significance of the happenings of the past. Accordingly, a historical ideal type is the result of one-sided accentuation and a systematic stylization of historical facts (Weber, *Objectivity*, p. 90). A historical ideal type is warped and lopsided, for it carries more logical consistency and less factual or historical detail than the reality it represents; and also because it favors certain elements of objective reality as "relevant" and "significant" to the exclusion of others. All ideal types reduce empirical reality to a utopian model in order to overcome the overwhelming multiplicity of the concrete data. Weber does not claim that the chosen facts are in any way more "essential," but rather they are more significant for the observers. Thus the selection of data organized in ideal types must not be regarded as an instance of arbitrarily simplifying the complexity of historical event (Weber, *Social*, p. 294). If our limitedness in time and space, and our particularity of interests is a disadvantage, Weber turns it into an advantage: we come to understand, not in spite of our prejudices but precisely because of them.[16] The liberating effect of this idea stems directly from a sense of modesty that underlies it. Weber took a bold step when he recognized that "our" history inevitably bears the imprint of our particular interest in it. Thus, he liberated sociologists as well as other social scientists and particularly historians from the burdensome pretension of German idealism, which required them to be selfless oracles of reason (or revolution). It also pulverized the puritanical obsession of French positivism with cleansing the mind of the social scientist from the contagion of values and interests.[17] The use of ideal types enables us to accept and utilize rather than to fight the fact that we confront our society and history as finite human beings whose interests define the past as much as they are defined by it.

The fact that for Weber the criterion of meaningfulness of ideal types is not the abstract and universal principle of logic but rather "subjective adequacy"—which amounts to agreement with "common sense,"[18]—also epitomizes the liberating modesty of his methodology:

> The interpretation of a coherent course of conduct is "subjectively adequate" (or "adequate on the level of meaning"), insofar as, ac-

cording to our habitual modes of thought and feeling, its component parts taken in their mutual relation are recognized to constitute a "typical" complex of meaning. It is more common to say "correct." (Weber, *Economy I*, p. 11)

An ideal type, therefore, is subjectively adequate as soon as it is constructed and as long as it meets Weber's rather modest criteria. Of course, there is no guarantee that "our habitual modes of thought and feeling" would reflect the truth. But, in Weber's view, embracing the metaphysical truth is not the goal for which sociology or any of the social sciences must strive. In no case, Weber argues, does the "meaning" sociology strives to apprehend (whether "actual existing"—concrete or average—or "the pure type") refer to an objectively "correct" meaning or one which is "true" in some metaphysical sense. Instead of verifying them we simply determine the empirical validity of the subjectively adequate ideal types by estimating the odds of their occurrence, i.e. their "causal adequacy." It is this which distinguishes the empirical sciences of action, such as sociology and history, from dogmatic disciplines such as jurisprudence, logic and aesthetics which seek to ascertain the "true" and "valid" meanings associated with the objects of their investigation (Weber, *Economy I*, p. 4).

In the realm of comparative sociology, which is indispensable for sociology of intellectuals, we need to deal with cultural concepts of alien civilizations. Although the prior distinction seems to relieve the social sciences from the task of judging the validity or legitimacy of other cultures, still a nonjudgmental understanding of alien cultures remains problematic.[19] One might ask if "*our* habitual modes of thought and feeling" can legitimately constitute the criterion for the subjective validity of ideal types; and if the guiding light for selection and definition of social problems also originates in "our" interests, would it not be impossible for the observer to reach an interpretive understanding of cultures other than one's own? How are we supposed to check the subjective adequacy of the ideal types we make about other cultures? How can we define their social problems? How do we select the "significant" facts from their history? The sociological study of alien cultures thus has to contend with the same problems that beset historical investigations.

The strength of Weber's response to both these problems lies in his bold recognition of the limits that human finitude imposes on knowledge. As a hermeneutical consciousness of our rootedness in time renders destructive prejudice into constructive historical insight, also an awareness of our defined presence in geocultural space can turn cultural distance into intellectual leverage for understanding. In studying the world of predecessors or in examining different layers of the world of contemporaries,[20] the human interests present a Janus face. While denial or self-righteous assertion of these interests greatly impedes understanding, an awareness of ones rootedness in time and space turns the blind spot of human particularity into a lens for scientific, that is, selective and discriminating, study of empirical reality. Hence Weber conceded that his theory of concept formation was "anthropomorphic" (Burger, p. 80). We can even call it "ethnocentric." But here, ethnocentrism, rather than being an expression of the self-righteousness of a dominant culture, testifies to the conscious adaptation of the science of man to the "human condition." Unless we have an "Archimedean point," i.e., a particular value-relevant (and scientific) interest, it becomes impossible for us to "scientifically" study any alien culture.[21] The subject of investigation therefore must be "valuable" for the social scientist.

This also holds true for the realm of history. The observer cannot help but look at history from his or her own point of view. The concept of "value relevance," however, transcends narrow utilitarian interests and individual biases. Weber rejected Mayer's restriction of the value-relevant interest of the historian only to effective history; that is to those historical elements that have been causally effective in bringing about the "present" (Weber, *Mayer*, p. 157). For Weber, even the most historically inconsequential facts of an alien civilization (e.g., those of the Incas and Aztecs) can become the subject of the value-relevant interest of the historian both as "heuristic instruments" for the formation of theoretical concepts appropriate to the study of culture as such,[22] and as "historical individuals" studied with respect to their "relevance to values"[23] (Weber, *Mayer*, p. 156). Weber's own attempts to come to grips with civilizational and historical complexes neither aimed at capturing their totality nor claimed to have reproduced the world view of their "natives." His main "interest" was to discover the role of the religiously grounded economic ethics of these civilizations.

He sought an answer to the following question (and this was his "Archimedean point"): Why did the causal nexus of events in these civilizations fail to produce "capitalism," which stood at the current end of the European historical development? Our aim in the present study is to examine the role of intellectuals in historically and geo-culturally distant times and places. In order to accomplish this we do not need to transcend history or culture, but only to erect a logically consistent (if culturally specific) structure for containing data about the role of intellectuals in (historically and geocul-turally) distant civilizations. In the case of the so-called cultural diffusion, intellectuals of these very civilizations have borrowed from each other.

In every case, from the extraordinary resistance of Judaism to elements of Egyptian and Babylonian neighbors to the easy spread of Hinduism in the subcontinent, the intellectuals have considered cultural products available for borrowing, in the light of their civilizational priorities as well as in view of their own ideal and material interests, before opting to adopt or reject them (Weber, *Judaism*, pp. 190, 203–205; *India*, pp. 9, 16). There is no reason to exclude the Western scientific process from this practice. The last important caveat about the ideal types is that:

3. *Ideal types do not subsume reality. It is the reality that approximates the ideal types.* We have already mentioned that the adequacy at the level of meaning of an ideal type must be complemented by measuring its causal adequacy:

> The interpretation of a sequence of events will . . . be called *causally* adequate insofar as, according to established generalizations from experience, there is a probability that it will always actually occur in the same way. (Weber, *Economy I*, p. 11)

This, however, does not mean that ideal types must be "validated" or "verified" in the same way that hypotheses are verified in the natural sciences. Ideal types are unlike the hypotheses of the natural sciences, as conceived by English empiricists since Bacon; ideal types are not premature theories. The construction of "general theories" (e.g., the rationalistic ideal types of typical action) in the social and cultural sciences is not the ultimate goal of these disciplines; the theories are mere instruments in achieving "the knowledge of the concrete reality."[24] The same is true for the historical ideal types.[25] Obviously both historical and sociological ideal types can assume the form of lawlike statements. This is only apparent. Sociological ideal types are not the result of an inductive verification of hypotheses. Indeed, they are nothing but the elaboration of a set of "teleological" or "dogmatically" ascribed assumptions. Those social scientists who insist on enthroning these ideal types as "laws of social and economic behavior" not only reject the centrality of the concrete reality as the subject matter of social sciences but also delude themselves about the origin of these so-called laws.[26] In summary, ideal types are neither overreaching laws nor all-embracing logical definitions.[27] The main function of an ideal type is to provide a basis for comparison:

> Its function is the comparison with empirical reality in order to establish its divergences or similarities, to describe them with the *most unambiguously intelligible concepts*, and to understand and explain them causally. (Weber, *Meaning*, p. 43)

Therefore, the logical parallel of ideal typical analysis is neither inductive nor deductive and not even analogical reasoning.[28] The use of ideal types rather resembles a simple rhetorical use of analogies. Except that here the example (ideal type) is not borrowed ready made, but is meticulously reconstructed through selection of the most "relevant" features of the reality. In this sense ideal types are "exemplary." An example cannot be verified or falsified. It only can be judged as subtle, relevant, and appropriate or otherwise, crude, irrelevant, and inappropriate.[29]

An ideal type is a measuring device, a "precision instrument." It is absurd to attempt to prove or disprove the measuring rod. One can only use one in order to determine how the reality "measures up" to it (Weber, *Stammler*, p. 111). It is a heuristic device for framing hypotheses (Weber, *Stammler*, p. 113). The ideal type is a model of meaning that the observer associates (Weber, *Stammler*, p. 111) with the action that is either historically observed or theoretically possible (Weber, *Logos*, p. 160).[30]

Although actual research is not meant to confirm or refute the ideal type, in the course of empirical research we can and constantly do judge the relevance and sensitivity of our ideal types. A search for confirmation (or refutation) of the ideal type is as meaningless as trying to validate the yardstick by seeking objects that are exactly one yard long. The question therefore is not whether the ideal type holds but to what extent it does. In ideal typical analysis we must ask how does the actual data approximate the meaning we have arrived at either by historical stylization or through a one-sided "rationalistic" and "teleological" ratiocination. We do not ask whether or not our ideal type is valid; rather the question is, how must the action proceed if the conduct is to correspond to the ideal type? Thus, Weber does not claim to know how a particular person "will" or should act but only how he "must" act in order for his conduct to correspond to the respective ideal type of action we have constructed (Weber, *Stammler*, p. 111).

It is only in the light of these considerations that the following passage of *Roscher and Knies*, in which Weber contrasts the hypotheses of natural sciences to ideal types, can be properly understood:

> A hypothetical "law of nature" which is definitively refuted in a *single* case collapses as an hypothesis once and for all. In contrast, the *idealtypical* constructions of economics—if they are correctly understood—have no pretensions at all to *general* validity. A "law of nature", on the other hand, *must* claim to be generally valid. Otherwise it loses its meaning. (Weber, *Knies*, p. 190)

The question, then, is to what extent the actual conduct corresponds to this rational scheme. Take the example of "Gresham's law" in economics. It is

> a rationally clear interpretation of human action under certain conditions and under the assumption that it will follow a purely rational course. How far any actual course of action corresponds to this can be verified only by the available statistical evidence for the actual disappearance of under-valued monetary units from circulation. (Weber, *Economy I*, p. 10)

Weber suggested that an unreal world of ideal types be constructed, in order to order scientifically the actual existing world. One-sidedly stylized, teleological, and rationalistic in nature, ideal types are but "utopian" models that have only instrumental value in attaining the goal of cultural sciences: the knowledge of concrete reality. Ideal types are not skeletons around which the reality should be formed; they are scaffolds that are discarded as soon as they fulfill their function. To do otherwise, e.g., to treat ideal types as the general theories of the natural sciences, would be to reify (Weber, *Stammler*, pp. 113–114) this fictitious world of images and examples. This is how we use ideal types in the present study: only as vessels whose actual utility must be examined in the process of actual research. Weber's theory of ideal types enables him to refer to such concepts as "the religion of intellectuals," "rationalization of magic in India," and "the Chinese patrimonial bureaucracy" without violating his methodological individualism. The constitutive role assigned to the value-relevant interest of the investigator in the construction of ideal types justifies differences of perspective and guarantees the open-ended reconstruction of the sociohistorical phenomena in the social sciences. The present study has benefited from this methodological argument in suggesting new ideal types such as "Religion for the Masses," as well as in recasting and restructuring the existing ideal types in new configurations.

On Human Interest and Historical Causation

What is historical causation? A solid objective chain of events or a subjectively reconstructed affair mediated by subjective considerations (interests, values, cultural categories, etc.) of the historian? By the turn of the century, "intuitionism" and "historical materialism" had provided the most distinct answers to these question. The famous debate between the two schools had so charged the atmosphere that neutral historical research could not have been conducted without taking a position on this debate. Weber opted to propose his own solution. His response is of central importance to our project because one of the most tenacious problems of sociology of intellectuals is to determine their role in creating as well as in recapitulating the historical process.

Weber settled the problems of "historical determination" and "historical interest" by linking the two together through the category of "objective possibility." We have already pointed out that

Weber's notion of historical interest was much broader than that of his contemporary, Eduard Mayer, who confined it to the discovery of the causal sequence of historical events that had brought about "the present" (Weber, *Mayer*, pp. 153-156). Yet from Mayer, Weber seems to have appropriated the method of "ascent from effect to cause": "The totality of all conditions back to which the causal chain from the "effect" leads had to "act jointly in a certain way and in no other for the concrete effect to be realized" (Weber, *Mayer*, p. 187). By definition every historical happening, without exception, is "necessitated" by a countless number of historical "causes." A historian who follows the causes down to a certain effect is apt to imagine the outcome was "necessitated" from the outset. Such a methodology will lead to an optical illusion: the vision of a teleologically moving specter replaces history. Weber's reversal of the direction of research (from effects to causes not the other way around) together with his alternative concept of historical determination (adequate causation) avoids the deterministic fallacy. Weber's notion of historical determination, for instance, incorporates the possibility of "historical accidents." The problem with this approach is that it is neither possible nor desirable to track "all" of the causes of an event (which are infinitely multiple). Weber's solution was to use the "historical interest" of the investigator as the criterion of selection of the relevant causes. Historical interest would orient the retrospective quest for those few "relevant" and "significant" causal connections that lay behind historical events (Weber, *Mayer*, pp. 151-152). But how can such a method avoid anthropomorphizing the history? How can we propose that the values of the historian govern the selection of data without turning history into an ever changing private tale of historians?

The answer is to be found in the proper use of the categories of "adequate causation" and "objective possibility" (Weber, p. 186). It was the utilization of these two concepts in the process of ascent from effects to the "significant" causes that enabled Weber to bypass many dangerous methodological rapids of materialistic or idealistic historical determination. How?

Historical causation for Weber is not a separate type of causation, it is objective causation viewed from the perspective of human interests.[31] To facilitate the conversion of "objective" into "historical" causation, Weber devised and used the categories of "objective possibility" and "adequate causation." They modify the historical interest of the investigator as it delves into the past in order to discern and scientifically arrange an array of facts and concepts that are "significant" from his point of view. In this manner the "value-relevant interest" of the investigator is converted into a scientific tool for recreating a scientific image of the past.

But first the fetish of an unchangeable past that confronts the historian as an "invincible rock" must be broken. Neither the advocates of ideal or material determinism nor the practitioners of traditional historiography are exempt from this challenge. Weber fought the tyranny of the past by cutting off the chain of events that seem to have "necessitated" a given historical happening. To solve this problem Weber invented what is now known as *counterfactual trajectories* in historiography in order to dissolve the solidity of history.

Starting with the question: "What would have happened if? . . ." the historian imagines alternative trajectories for the history. Of course it is the historical interest of the investigator that fills the dotted line and determines which link in the causal succession of causes leading to the event in question is to be hypothetically removed. For example, a political historian would be interested in estimating the historical significance of a voluntaristic decision of a political leader. In the realm of the sociology of knowledge the causal significance of ideas and in the sociology of intellectuals the role of the bearers of these ideas constitute the subject of interest. Therefore in the question "What would have happened if? . . ." it is always the subject of "interest" that is hypothetically removed from the causal chain leading to a historical event. Through this type of questioning a distance is created between the historical causes and their effects, allowing a certain leeway for exploration of possibilities and also for comparative historical analysis.

Now, if the answer to the counterfactual question is positive (i.e., that the event in question would still have happened without "this particular" link), it is to be inferred that the event in question had been "objectively possible" at the time it came to pass. Retrospectively we refer to such an event as having been "adequately caused." Such an event cannot be described as a "historical accident" even though it might appear to have been objectively triggered by a fortuitous event. In such a case the fortuitous character of the proximate cause is of no significance. Like the proverbial straw that breaks the camel's back, like the "last turn of the screw," such an immediate cause merely happens to "necessitate" an event that would in all probability materialize in any case. Such an event is "adequately caused"; it is not an instance of "historical accident." From the point of view of the present time, a future development can be called "objectively possible" only when we have evidence that it is on the verge of happening and a further regular accumulation of events "in its favor" including sheer accidents might well "necessitate" it or hasten its materialization.[32]

The logical opposite of an adequately caused event is a "historical accident." To subsume a sudden turn of events under this category it is not enough for its proximate cause to be a "fortuitous" one. An event qualifies as a historical accident when it could be said of it that it would never have happened in any shape or form had the immediate fortuitous cause not been present. For the contemporaries of the historical event in question, the objective possibility of a historical accident is nil. To put it in a more anthropomorphic language, when an event happens without having a considerable array of other events weighing on its side, we say it is not "adequately caused"; it is a "historical accident."[33]

The task of determining the type of causation involved in a given historical development is entrusted to the empirical research guided by the historical interests of the investigator who weighs the relative significance of certain historical causes leading up to the event in question.

In dealing with the interface of ideas and interests in history (e.g., in sociologies of knowledge and intellectuals) we are called upon to make judgments of this sort. One cannot answer this in metatheory. Each case must be decided on empirical grounds. In certain cases Weber refers to "concrete" historical or "accidental" determinants (Weber, *Judaism*, p. 167; *Economy I*, p. 40) of a historical configuration (Weber, *India*, p. 240), while on other occasions he calls an entire historical development a "historical accident." For instance, the spread of Buddhism to Southeast Asia is called by Weber a "historical accident" (Weber, *India*, p. 230). This obviously means that it was not an objectively possible development for Buddhism to spread beyond its original grounds. Such a development could therefore be judged to have been exclusively caused by the conversion of King Ashuka, who zealously sought to internationalize his religion. Here the proximate cause is the real one. On the other hand, Buddhism's active opposition to the ruling strata, although lacking in ancient Buddhism, was always a "latent possibility" in view of its denunciation of the Indian social order and of caste ritualism (Weber, *India*, p. 240). Thus, when actualized, the latter development cannot be called a "historical accident," because it was always "objectively possible."

In another example, Weber deems it entirely legitimate (although he does not take sides on this specific question) to argue that the assassination attempt that heralded the First World War be discarded as insignificant if it is sufficiently clear that the international situation of the time was volatile enough to be set ablaze by "any" spark (Weber, *Mayer*, p. 166). Knowing that the First World War was started by a Serbian student's bullet tells us nothing about whether it was "historical accident." The sociology of intellectuals must make these types of judgments whenever intellectuals advance a historically consequential "ideology." These questions cannot be settled ahead of time in a metatheoretical argument but must be resolved in the process of field research.

On Social Change

A Weberian answer to the question: "How is history possible?" can be provided on the basis of the categories of "objective possibility" and "adequate causation," which integrate human interest into, and recognize it as an integral part of, the methodology of historical sciences. What would be left of a given "historical development" if we were to deprive ourselves of the advantage of human perspective? Weber's view of the "objective" direction or mechanics of historical change as reflected in his theory of "social selection," while resembling the approach of social Darwinism or that of the theories of social conflict, is devoid of their melioristic or rationalizing overtones. For one thing, Weber does not assume that the outcome of social conflict or competition is always determined by the intrinsic superiority of the surviving individuals, groups, or sociocultural forms. "Survival" can be the result of quite concrete extrinsic historical circumstances or "accidents." The deciding factor in "social selection" is the "differential advantage" of the surviving groups or forms, which is not necessarily indicative of "fitness to survive" or of a superior "adaptedness," but can result from any number of social or natural changes. Survival may also be an unintended consequence of actions of any of the parties involved in the "competitive struggle" (Weber, *Economy I*, pp. 38–40).

Weber considered the use of concepts such as "fitness to survive" or "adaptedness," which had become popular in the wake of biologically imbued theories of evolution, to be begging the question and charged with surreptitious value judgments. He declared: "The fact that a given specific social relationship has been eliminated for reasons peculiar to a particular situation, proves nothing whatever about its 'fitness to survive' in general terms" (Weber, *Economy I*, p. 40). A close examination of the belief that fitness to survive alone accounts for survival shows that it is a close relative of the deterministic fallacy, which Weber avoided by suggesting that the flow of reasoning be revised (from effects to causes not vice versa). "The totality of 'all' the conditions back to which the causal chain from the 'effect' leads had to 'act jointly' in a certain way and in no other for the concrete effect to be realized" (Weber, *Mayer*, p. 187). In the same vein the survival of a group or a social form can be adequately or accidentally caused by a number of intrinsic qualities, extrinsic circumstances, intended as well as unintended consequences of human action. To conveniently simplify this complex process by stating that only the fittest will survive is to reduce the science of history to fallacy: only the fittest survive; anything that survived must have been fit!

In censuring another aspect of social Darwinism and evolutionism invoked in the ideology of modern technocratic elites, Weber's critique aims at the logical foundations as well as the ideological ramifications of the concept of "adaptedness":

Strictly and exclusively empirical analysis can provide a solution only where it is a question of a means adequate to the realization of an absolutely unambiguously given end. The proposition: x is the only means by which y can be attained, is in fact merely the reverse of the proposition: y is the effect of x. The term "adaptedness" (and all

other related terms) do not provide—and this is the main thing—
even the slightest hint about the value-judgments which they contain
and which they actually obscure. . . . Depending on how one uses the
term, either everything or nothing in society is "adapted." (Weber,
Meaning, p. 26)

Weber was especially weary of value judgments implicit in major
theories of social change. The use of the concept of "progress"
characterizing the inevitable benignity of the evolution of mankind
could not be condoned by Weber. He maintained that the word
"progress" be legitimately applied only in a nonevaluative context
where it signifies the "'continuation' of some concrete process of
change viewed in isolation" (Weber, *Meaning*, p. 27). For instance,
progress in the realm of art can be discerned not in its aesthetic or
evaluative sense but only with regard to "the technical means which
a certain type of artistic impulse applies when the end is definitely
given" (Weber, *Meaning*, p. 29).

In the realm of social psychology also, one could elaborate on an
objective process of progressive differentiation "in the 'scope' or
'capacity' of a concrete 'mind,'" but, Weber added, "whether one
designates progressive differentiation as 'progress' is a matter of
terminological convenience" (Weber, *Meaning*, pp. 27, 28). In a yet
different level of analysis, Weber advanced beyond exposing the
fallacies as well as evaluative undercurrents in the theories of "progress" and questioned their single-minded optimism:

Whoever wishes to state a value-judgment regarding the fact of
differentiation as such—which no empirical discipline can forbid—
and seeks a point of view from which this can be done, will come
upon the question as to the price which is "paid" for the process.
(Weber, *Meaning*, p. 28)

Compared with the theories of evolution (and, in particular,
social Darwinism), Weber's theory of social selection is "value
neutral" and nonteleological. But it is also true that it lays no claim
to have explanatory or predictive powers. Nor does it presume to
scientifically arrive at practical social policies. Yet it is far from pure
mental exercise. Indeed, Weber's theory is a parody of the objective
theories of social change and as such it serves pedagogical purposes.

It can be perceived as a tool for weaning the social sciences from prematurely imposed patterns of change and warning them against the false sense of security such theories impart.

It must also be noted that our critique of the theories that subsume Weber as a "conflict sociologist" is not meant to deny the universal significance of the concept of conflict in Weber's world view. Weber perceived the world as an utterly unrationalizable conglomerate of contradictions among, as well as within, the spheres of life.[34] Only when this is accepted as an ontological axiom would it follow that the sole corresponding theological depiction of such a world must be polytheistic, recognizing as inevitable the irreconcilable and uncompromising death struggles between the gods (Weber, *Meaning*, p. 17; *Politics*, p. 123). Weber observed that attempts at transcending these contradictions in thought have time and again produced the reverse effect. By drawing attention to the problems they attempt to solve, such overly rationalized images of the world are likely to rob people of the only protective shield they wear against the disturbing influence of the contradictions of their world: their ignorance of them (Weber, *Meaning*, p. 18). The rule of thumb here is: The more rationally consistent a theoretical image of the world, the more useless it becomes (Weber, *Social*, p. 275; *Economy I*, p. 526). In the religious sphere, therefore, the theoretical rationalization of the world image comes into conflict with the primitive practical rationalization of the religious life. As the former increasingly favors radical abnegation of the world for its recalcitrant refusal to evince the meaning it is supposed to contain, the latter's conciliatory and piecemeal approach to the problems of evil and meaninglessness in the world is condemned and pushed aside (Weber, *Economy I*, p. 424; *Rejections*, p. 355).

In the sphere of political ethics, Weber rejected as naive and ultimately dangerous the monism of the "cosmic ethical 'rationalist'" who disregards the eternal and unresolvable conflict of ethical maxims (Weber, *Politics*, pp. 122–123; *Meaning*, pp. 15, 16). Therefore the intellectualistic, overly rationalized image of the world is declared by Weber to be unfit for practical and political action, as it is bound to foster dogmatic adherence to the "ethics of ultimate" ends and generate political irresponsibility.[35] The logical opposite of this world view, which Weber seems to recommend to the politicians, is a warrior's ethic of following only one's own god or demon, of heroically confronting one's fate in an irrational world of many deities (Weber, *India*, p. 27; *Social*, p. 283).

Despite Weber's commitment to a philosophy of eternal conflict, however, he never hypostatized it as the "driving force" or the "pivot" of objective social change. On the sociological plane Weber deemed conflict to be both ineradicable and ubiquitous (Weber, *Economy I*, p. 39). But the fact that conflict can be properly defined only when the intentionality of concrete actors is concerned (and this is consonant with Weber's methodological individualism) disqualifies conflict as the determinant of the direction of social change. For Weber, the scope of social conflict is rather limited because it can account for social change only insofar as such change originates in conflictual or competitive social action. Conflict is only one among many necessary components of Weber's theory of social change. In an exceptionally revealing passage, Dahrandorf uses an analogy likening the social conflict view of the society to a hyperbola, while the model of the integration or consensus theories is said to be an elliptical one (Dahrandorf, *Social Conflict*, p. 106). Weber's image of society and especially his theory of social selection are far too complex and multifocal to resemble any of the aforementioned geometrical models. Conflict of various status groups or classes that make up the society, their various "ways of life" that constitute the "culture," and their competitive struggle for social and cultural predominance are rightly depicted by Bendix to characterize Weber's anticollectivistic view of the subject matter of sociology (Bendix, 1977, p. 261). But the theory of social selection recognizes conflict and competition only as two spokes not the hub of the turning wheel of history. They are indispensable to but not exclusively constitutive of social change. The following passage, often quoted by the followers of the conflict school of thought (Coser, 1956, p. 21), indicates only the indispensability of conflict, not its centrality to Weber's theory of social change.

> Conflict cannot be excluded from social life. One can change its means, its object, even its fundamental direction and its bearers, but it cannot be eliminated . . . "peace" is nothing more than a change in the form of the conflict or in the antagonists or in the objects of the conflict, or finally in the chances of selection. (Weber, *Meaning*, pp. 26–27)

As all (intentional) action leading to change, conflict-oriented and competitive action are also liable to be undone by their own unintended consequences. Even accidental natural and social changes can intervene to create certain "differential advantages," which may, despite all rationally directed conflictual and competitive action, decide which group or class survives. The concept of conflict, as an inseparable part of the process of social selection, refers to action oriented intentionally to carrying out the individual actor's own will against the resistance of the other party or parties. A peaceful and regulated conflict is called "competition." As opposed to conflict and competition, "social selection" does not require the intentional predisposition of the social actors: "the struggle, often latent, which takes place between human individuals or social types, for advantages and for survival, but without a meaningful mutual orientation in terms of conflict will be called selection" (Weber, *Economy I*, p. 38).

Social "selection" and "social conflict" must be ascribed to social relationships as far as the probabilities of meaningful action on the part of individual actors (be it a conscious effort against the will of others or mere struggle to achieve personal goals) are concerned. But can we also conceive of conflict between social relationships (as most theorists of conflict have done), or of social selection among them? Weber rejects this formally but condones its metaphorical use (Weber, *Economy I*, p. 39) as long as the following is kept in perspective: "This so called 'selection' has nothing to do with the selection of types of human individuals" (Weber, *Economy I*, p. 40).

Weber favored the use of the metaphor of selection instead of that of conflict for describing the "objective" process of social change. The lack of the axiom of mutual intentional predisposition of the actors in social selection allows a certain leeway for the exploration of individual cases where the significance of the intentionally oriented action varies greatly. Social conflict may or may not be decisive in determining the outcome of social selection depending on the individual cases. Social selection, therefore, is a blind mechanism; it has a logic but no teleology. When understood in human terms, it might be studied as a selective fulfillment of an assortment of objective possibilities. Like overly rational theodicies of evil, the theory of social selection that accounts for all of the accidental and rational elements is rendered useless.[36] Weber's theory is such a theory: uselessness is its goal.

One can think of Weber's theory of social selection as a "transitional object," a pacifier of sorts that helps one unlearn the habit of seeking patterns in the past. Although it first appears to be an objective philosophy of history, once understood it collapses into itself and reveals that it can not generate a theory of social change, let alone a philosophy of history. The sterility of the theory of social selection mirrors the penury of any "objective" theory of social change if it is stripped of hidden value judgments and mystifying circular logic. The shadowy presence of the theory of social selection in Weber's sociology of intellectuals is felt more as a neutral ether to prevent erroneous conjectures than as a positive theory of social change. As in other fields of sociology, Weber's methodology helps one to turn to empirical research rather than to seek answers in philosophical conjecture. It helps one to avoid pitfalls rather than provide a guide to the correct path.

2

Max Weber's Sociology of Religion as a Sociology of Intellectuals

Marx and Weber on Intratheoretical Consistency: Sociologies of Knowledge and Intellectuals

Like the theme of rationality in Weber's works, the sociology of intellectuals is a pervasive motif, not a distinct aspect of his sociology. Sociology of intellectuals is nevertheless a substantively rich and theoretically fecund region of Weber's universe of discourse, and we hope to demonstrate this by reconstructing it in this book. The most salient feature of Weber's sociology of intellectuals is its extraordinary lucidity exactly in the areas where alternative attempts (namely those of the Marxist school) have produced only obscure or obscurantist formulations.

This chapter is based on the assumption that the consistency of Weber's epistemological stance with his sociology of knowledge and their joint contribution to his substantive sociologies of religion and politics are responsible for the clarity of pivotal definitions and explanations upon which a sociology of intellectuals is built. Of course, such consistency, desired as it may be, is neither necessary nor sufficient for the constitution of a viable theory of intellectuals. Indeed, the study of the Marxist theory of intellectuals demonstrates that a degree of intratheoretical ambiguity between the spheres of epistemology, sociology of knowledge, and sociology of intellectuals can spark many intriguing debates among the protagonists of various versions of "the real intent" of the texts in question. This has led to a sharp delineation of the tensions and problems that had been neglected by Marx. We intend to start this chapter by comparing and contrasting Weber's views on sociology of religion to those of Marx and Marxists in order to highlight the role of intratheoretical consistency (lack thereof) in the study of sociologies of religion and of intellectuals. Then we will continue by reconstructing a series of ideal types for the religions of various classes and strata and by contrasting these religious needs to those of intellectuals.

To consider Marxist and sociological texts as integral parts of the sociology of intellectuals requires the adoption of a broader perspective than that provided by the conventional standards of either discourse. Transcending the field-specific jargon of both fields will reveal that the two disciplines constitute parallel universes; that for every argument and counterargument concerning the role of intellectuals in one there is an analogous debate in the other. A comparative study in parallel fields of sociology and Marxism will underline the importance of intratheoretical consistency for the clear formulation of a sociology of intellectuals.

In comparing the two fields one will also find that academic sociology's discussion of intellectuals, sedate as it might appear at the outset, does not entirely lack the liveliness and enthusiasm with which similar questions are discussed by Marxist theorists. In fact, such forerunners of sociology of intellectuals as Karl Mannheim and Emile Lederer, who contributed to the establishment of sociology of intellectuals as an independent branch of sociology, had more than dispassionate academic interest in the subject (Mannheim, 1936; Lederer, 1940). Indeed, like some of their Marxist counterparts, they sought to find an ideology for, rather than a sociology of, intellectuals (Mannheim, 1943). For many other sociologists, constructing a scientific theory of intellectuals has posed the challenge of ultimate reflexivity; for those with platonic complexes or ambitions it has become a fount of profound self-doubt and a source of legitimation crises.

Weber viewed the question of intellectuals with both passion and perspective. His sociology of religion reflects his theoretical interest in the matter; his political sociology reveals his ideological interests, his hopes, fears, and worries regarding the future of his civilization. Weber dedicated two of his most profound lectures to the pure calling of a scientist and the political mission of a citizen/intellectual (Weber, *Science*; *Politics*). Before substantively discussing these themes, however, we must recognize that it was Weber's intratheoretical consistency that allowed him to lucidly debate these issues.

The vagueness of Marx's sociology of knowledge leaves his sociology of intellectuals virtually eclipsed: What is the relation of ideas to social reality? What is the status of the carriers of ideas in the social system? Do they create ideas independently, or simply reflect class contradictions? Must they lead the progressive movement of the society, or should they only observe and follow? The subsequent acrimonious debate regarding these questions among his followers is indicative of Marx's fundamental ambivalence. However, eliminating contradictions and imparting theoretical clarity have rarely been the driving force behind these vitriolic debates. Rather, theorists of the left have debated the role of intellectuals in relation to its practical value for socialist movements. Rosa Luxemburg considered the resolution of the ideological controversy over the role of party "intellectual" in the workers' struggle as vital for the very survival of the global revolutionary movement of which she was a part (Luxemburg, 1990). Lenin, her theoretical opponent, having actually led the first successful Bolshevik revolution did not attach less importance to the question of the role of intellectuals (inside and outside the party). Hence, the famous indirect debate between the two (Lenin, 1973).

Only the later academically oriented Marxists have attempted to treat the question of intellectuals with a consideration for consistency of the axioms of sociologies of knowledge and intellectuals. Among the latter, Alvin Gouldner, a self-professed left Hegelian, is a major case in point.

He took the Marxist axiom of the social determination of consciousness and seriously tried to construct a sociology of intellectuals on that basis. What he discovered was that the left Hegelian legacy had been betrayed by its most famous heir: Marx. The Marxist sociology of intellectuals, Gouldner observed, is based not only on ignorance and false consciousness but also on deception and distortion (Gouldner, 1979, pp. 9, 11, 57, 85). Postulating a strictly Marxist sociology of knowledge endowed Gouldner with a keen eye for recognizing "ideologies" of intellectuals masquerading as transcendental voices of reason or revolution. The following example will illustrate that, indeed, intellectuals' zeal for intratheoretical consistency might radically undermine an ideological system rather than furthering its development and refinement. Philosophical Marxism maintains that the proletariat is the sole subject and the "we" of history. Gouldner doubts that Marx ever believed this. He quotes the passage in which Marx seems to have subscribed to the idea: "We expressly formulate the battle cry: the emancipation of the working class must be conquered by the working class themselves"; but, Gouldner interdicts, "Who was the we who formulated the battle cry?" (Gouldner, p. 75).

Let us venture beyond recognizing the contradiction in order to locate its roots. The penury of Marx's sociology of knowledge has allowed the axiom of the social determination of knowledge to degenerate into a kind of reductionism that Marx seemed more eager to defend than to disavow. The decisive role that Marxism assigns to an advanced proletariat in breaking through "the antinomies of bourgeois thought," as reflected upon by George Lukacs in the problem of "labor-time," carries the implication that contemplative intellectualization cannot by itself achieve the knowledge of the social totality, let alone constitute a basis for revolutionary praxis in order to change it (Lukacs, 1971, pp, 167–172). The knowledge of the totality is held to flow from the immediate experience of time spent under the conditions of exploitation not the time spent on tomes of scientific analysis of it. Couple these observations with the aversion of "committed thinkers" toward the irresponsibility of pure "seekers of pure knowledge," and that of the left toward inherently untrustworthy "bourgeois intellectuals," and one has reasons enough to account for Marx's lack of interest in elaborating the role of intellectuals in effecting the socialist transformation. Marx's blatant neglect of the issue deprived him of reflexivity, of, to quote Gouldner, "being able to account for himself."

Marx, preferred to defer the issue indefinitely. But Lenin's historical role compelled him to tackle the problem more explicitly. Rather than offering a theoretical resolution, however, Lenin concentrated on practical necessities such as the fundamental indispensability of the intellectual core of the workers' movement: the party. Lenin preferred to dodge the class analysis of ideas and ideologies and to avoid invoking the Marxist principle of the social determination of consciousness. With an odd mixture of ingeniousness and political shrewdness he also suspended the typical Marxist suspicion about the motives of those intellectuals who became "professional revolutionaries."

What did all this mean? Why would bourgeois intellectuals renounce their own class and not only join but also lead members of an opposing class to victory against their own class? Having made history, Lenin was not too keen on justifying his theoretical gambits. His socialist opponents could fuss over these weak theoretical links in what appeared to be an enormous practical success, and the debate continued for decades. Sociology of ideas (knowledge) and their carriers (intellectuals) needs a solid theoretical standpoint, which is lacking in Marxism.

The flourishing of Weber's sociology of religion, his political sociology, and, of course, the clarity of his sociology of intellectuals are all due to his clear stance regarding the interplay of ideas and interests in the sphere of the sociology of knowledge. The postulation of relatively autonomous spheres for ideas and interests, which also led Weber to oppose the attempts of dogmatic historical materialists to trace all ideas (including religious ones) back to the economic infrastructure, allowed for the free exploration of the dialectics of ideas and interests. This is best illustrated, for example, by the basic concepts upon which Weber constructed his sociology of religion.

Marx and Weber on Sociology of Religion

The widespread acceptance of proto-Marxist historical materialism among his contemporaries (e.g., Kautsky) inspired Weber to attempt a clandestine refutation of that school. This "debate with the ghost of Marx" consists of a series of scattered and indirect but persistent refutations of historical materialism. Thus, Weber refused to assume that "the specific nature of a religion is a simple 'function' of the social situation of the stratum which appears as its characteristic bearer, or that it represents the stratum's ideology, or that it is a 'reflection' of a stratum's material or ideal interest situation" (Weber, *Social*, pp. 269–270). In other words, "the nature of a stratum's religiosity has nowhere been solely determined by economic conditions" (Weber, *China*, p. 196). He maintained that even when the influence of economic factors in the religious sphere is obvious, still "the idiosyncratic autonomy of the religious domain" remains ascendant (Weber, *Economy I*, p. 433). Weber's methodological stance is clear: he espoused the relative autonomy of the sphere of ideas. The Weberian sociology of knowledge does contain allusions to "affinities" between ideas and economic constellations (Weber, *Economy I*, p. 480), the "wedding" of certain thought products and a particular social order, (Weber, *India*, p. 131) and at times allows for a "co-determination" of the content of religion by extra religious factors (Weber, *Judaism*, p. 80; *China*, p, 249). But Weber never "explained" religious phenomena as economic products or vice versa.

According to Weber, the prohibition of usury by the Catholic church was not caused by the absence of interest on capital under the natural economy, as was claimed by the proponents of historical materialism. He noted that the church, and even the Pope himself, partook in unscrupulous usury during the Middle Ages. The prohibition of usury was a later phenomenon: the result of the consummation of the process of theoretical rationalization of the religious domain (Weber, *Economy I*, p. 584). Weber advanced a similar argument to refute the materialistic explanation of the origin of Jainism in India. Although Jainism originated at the time of the rise of the Indian city and was enthusiastically received in the new urban centers, it was not "a 'product' of the 'bourgeoisie,'" rather, "it stemmed from Kshatriya speculation and lay asceticism" (Weber, *India*, p. 202). Weber also refused to treat Jewish prophecy in terms of the economic infrastructure. Jewish prophets came from diverse origins (Weber, *Judaism*, p. 277), he pointed out, yet they often conveyed a similar message, addressing the negatively privileged and uneducated strata. Their prophecy of doom was hardly marketable, and their intellectual efforts went unremunerated (Weber, *Economy I*, p. 441). Despite ties to the traditional intelligentsia, they fought against the dominant cultured strata and prophets of good fortune, as well as their patrons, the Jewish kings (Weber, *Judaism*, pp. 109, 278).

A careful reading of Weber will reveal that he did not intend to "substitute for a one sided materialistic an equally one sided spiritualistic causal interpretation of culture and history" (Weber,

Protestant, p. 183). Weber maintained that religion can play a significant role in economic change only when powerful drives toward an economic transformation are also present in the existing constellation of relationships and interests (Weber, *Economy I*, p. 577). He expressed his position in the well-known passage: "Not ideas, but material interests, directly govern men's conduct. Yet very frequently the 'world images' that have been created by 'ideas' have, like switchmen, determined the tracks along which action has been pushed by the dynamic of interest" (Weber, *Social*, p. 280). If, when, where, and how an idea or its reinterpretation might come to determine the trajectory of history was deemed by Weber to be a matter of empirical research, it could not be deduced from any set of overreaching axiomatic or evolutionary laws (Weber, *Economy I*, p. 480).

Although Weber criticized those theorists who were in the habit of automatically assuming materialistic bases for any historically significant set of ideas, he did not exclude, in the name of methodological principles, the possibility of a "materialistic" explanation of an idea. Indeed, Weber did occasionally offer certain explanations that were not far from theories of historical materialism. For example, he argued that the existence of irrigation systems in Mesopotamia and Arabia was probably one source of the notion of a god who had created the earth and man out of nothing, rather than by procreating them (Weber, *Economy I*, p. 449). Moreover, he attributed the religious disinclination of the modern bourgeois and proletarian classes to the fact that they are no longer dependent on the course of natural and meteorological processes (Weber, *Economy I*, p. 485). Finally, Weber went beyond observing an affinity between organismic social theories and those socioeconomic circumstances that give rise to various forms of a "welfare state." Recognizing that socioeconomic and consequently political structures can determine the contours of social philosophy, he generalized about various philosophical legitimations of the welfare state: "Naturally such ideas suggest themselves to any political welfare organization" (Weber, *India*, p. 143; *Judaism*, pp. 257–258). In other words, ideologies of intelligentsia entrenched in patrimonial bureaucracies converged on the idea of state interventionism in the name of material or spiritual welfare of the masses, regardless of their civilizational differences (we will come back to this issue in Chapter 3).

The Marxist sociology of religion, in so far as it exists, is a sociology of mass religiosity. Even in this area Weber's observations are far more elegant compared with those of Marx. This is partly due to Marx's lack of interest in religion. The young Marx had of course reflected on the origin of religion and what it represented, but that he lacked interest (both personal and philosophical) in religion is evident in his later writings. After all, this problem had already been obsessively explored by one of his predecessors, namely, Feuerbach. In contrast to Feuerbach, Weber, not touching on the question of the origin of religious ideas, pursued a sociology of religion that focused on the interplay of religious ideas, on the one hand, and the interests of various social strata and classes, on the other. Hence, the Marxist sociology of religion overlaps certain aspects of Weber's, allowing for the claim that Weber's orientation embraced and elaborated ideas on the subject that Marx had developed earlier.[1]

In view of the fact that Marx's sketchy remarks on the social implications of religion have lent themselves to a variety of interpretations, ranging from a Leninist conspiracy theory of religion to Bloch's Marxist theology, is it necessary to qualify the preceding? We think not, because Weber's sociology of religion is wide enough to include, and broad enough to anticipate, the many interpretations of Marx. Consider the two aforementioned extremes of the Marxist sociology of religion: Lenin's conspiracy theory of religion versus Bloch's Marxist theology.

Lenin's militant antireligious attitude has a dual root, one of which is his admittedly eighteenth-century atheism; this is not at issue here. The second is his reductionist sociology of religion, which is inspired by Marx's statement: "Religion is the opium of the people." By this Lenin meant that in the hands of the exploiters religion is a mere instrument for stupefying and eventually oppressing the masses (Lenin, 1935, pp. 7, 12, 14, 45, 46). This line of reasoning, which became very prevalent in the wake of the success of the Russian Revolution, was later challenged by a number of heterodox Marxist interpreters. Ernst Bloch denounced the legacy of eighteenth-century "bourgeois philistines," holding it to be nothing more than "banal atheism" masquerading as the Marxist theory of religion (Bloch, 1970, p. 37). Attempts were also made to demystify Lenin's slogan by restoring it within the original context of

Marx's critique of Hegel's philosophy of law: "Religious distress is at the same time the expression of real distress and a protest against real distress. Religion is the sigh of the oppressed, the heart of the heartless world, just as it is the spirit of the spiritless situation. It is the opium of the people" (Marx, 1967, p. 250). Van Leeuwen warned that we must guard against distorting the phrase "opium of the people" into "opium for the people" (Van Leeuwen, 1972, p. 11).

Weber seems to have been aware of the "of and for" duality. He not only put forth the characteristics of "a religion of the people" in historical detail (in the manner of Bloch and Van Leeuwen) but also elucidated the formations and mechanisms that are associated with those constructed "for the people" in each historically specific situation. Weber's study of mass religiosity, therefore, covers both extremes of the Marxist theory of religion. This, however, is but one aspect of Weber's sociology of religion, as his reflections on the characteristics of the religiosity of intellectuals, warriors, and civic strata clearly demonstrate. The Weberian reflections on religions of various social classes and strata are based on a more fundamental concept of "religious needs."

Weber's basic postulation of the concept of religious needs is related to his thesis that "ideas" do not neatly intermesh with "interests" (Weber, *Social*, p. 268). If they do intermesh, the process is usually mediated by a secondary intellectual activity called the "reinterpretation of ideas." Religious reinterpretations, Weber observed, "adjust the revelations to the needs of the religious community." If this (the reinterpretations of the revealed ideas) occurs "then it is at least usual that the religious doctrines are adjusted to the *religious needs*" (Weber, *Social*, p. 270). Weber's analysis of religion is not only based on "the metaphysical needs of human mind" but also on the ideological needs of various strata and classes:

> The kind of empirical state of bliss or experience of rebirth that is sought after as the supreme value by a religion has obviously and necessarily varied according to the character of the stratum which was foremost in adopting it. The chivalrous warrior class, peasants, business classes, and intellectuals with literary education have naturally pursued different religious tendencies. As will become evident,

these tendencies have not by themselves determined the psychological character of religion; they have, however, exerted a very lasting influence upon it. The contrast between warrior and peasant classes, and intellectual and business classes, is of special importance (Weber, *Social*, p. 279).

Some Marxist theorists have recognized a need to go beyond polemicizing against religion as a social force and have come to appreciate Weber's accomplishments in exploring the psychological significance of religion (Bloch, 1971, p. 79; Birnbaum, pp. 133–34). Yet Weber's treatment of religion as a response to the particular ideal and material interests of various classes and social strata still remains undiscovered by Marxist thinkers. Weber's approach in his search for the "religious needs" of different strata and classes could be instructive for those Marxist theorists who are interested in studying the ideological nature of certain religious phenomena. Ideas and ideological needs, religions and religious needs fit together as a mortise and tenon joint; the study of one is inextricably bound to the learning of the other. The following examples shall demonstrate that when empirical evidence suggested, Weber did not shrink from offering classical materialistic interpretations about the origin of ideas.

Weber maintained, for instance, that the dependence of the peasants on organic processes and natural events and their distance from rational systematization of the economic life generate an inclination for animistic magic or ritualism as well as a resistance to ethical rationalization of the religious realm (Weber, *Economy I*, p. 468). He also concurred with Marx that the modern proletariat's dependence on purely social factors accounts for their indifference to or rejection of religion (Weber, *Economy I*, p. 485). Ideas can be autonomous from the material surroundings, but this is not necessarily the case.

Weber went beyond the sphere of mass religiosity. For instance, he considered the sphere of religious mythologies as a mirror reflecting social conflicts of various strata in the religious mythologies. Consider the following examples: for Weber the inferiority of the earth divinities to personal gods residing in clouds and mountains signified the triumph of knightly ethos over peasant religions (Weber, *Economy I*, p. 410). Also, the Vedic tension between Varuna and Mitra, the guardians of the sacred order, on one side, and Indra, a formidable warrior-god, on the other, was taken as an indication of the conflict between "the priesthood, striving for a firm regulation and control of life, and the powerful warlike nobility" (Weber, *Economy I*, p. 417). The ascension of celestial or astral gods in the pantheon not only reflected "the priesthood's propagation of systematized sacred ordinances," which would ensure the fixation of morality and judicial decisions, it would also rationalize the subordination of subjects to their overlords (Weber, *Economy I*, pp. 410, 417). Weber viewed the occidental religions with a similar theoretical bent, observing that the concept of Yahweh had changed from a war god to a city-dwelling, wise governor of the universe in order to accommodate the religious conceptions of the leading strata in various periods of Jewish history (Weber, *Judaism*, p. 133).

Despite the richness of Weber's observations regarding the religious needs of the urban masses, the peasantry, the warriors, the bureaucrats, and the various types of intellectuals, he did not attempt a formal classification of these ideal typical constructions because such a project would have been of secondary importance in view of his particular interest in world religions: that is, their relative conduciveness to capitalism. Yet, a rather basic class-oriented categorization of religious needs is legitimate and necessary for the purposes of the present study: a religion of intellectuals can be most fruitfully studied only in contrast to religions of other classes and strata. We will start with the study of mass religiosity. In order to bring to a close the series of comparisons between Marx and Weber, we will couch Weber's observation in this area in terms of the Marxist debate over religions of/for the masses.

Religion of the Masses

A clear parallel can be discerned between two pairs of ideal types that Weber used to characterize the religious inclinations of the masses. On the one hand, mass religiosity is counterposed to the religion of the contemplative, ascetic or mystic virtuosos (Weber, *General*, p. 364; *Judaism*, p. 246; *Social*, pp. 287–290; *Rejections*, p. 343). On the other, religions of the community (including the cults of state, tribe, or kinsmen) are described as distinct from and generally unresponsive to the religious needs of the lay individuals (Weber, *Social*, p. 272). The similarity between the religious needs of the masses and those of the "individual" (e.g., need for personal explanation of specific misfortune, and a mechanism for reversing it), as listed by Weber, can be explained if we conceive of the mass as an unorganized aggregate of uneducated and often "religiously unmusical" individuals (Weber, *Rejections*, p. 289).

The individual needs for a personal theodicy and for concrete help while in distress are rarely met by the communal deities who are in the business of guaranteeing victory over the enemy, control of the meteorological conditions, and success in booty and the hunt. Hence, the immense popularity of the sorcerers who catered to the needs of the individuals irrespective of their communal affiliations; a popularity that could potentially transcend local boundaries and provide for a transnational community of the devotees. In this process the sorcerers can develop into mystagogues and even prophets (Weber, *Social*, p. 277; *Judaism*, p. 166). It is in this sense that Weber claimed: "The magician has been the historical precursor of the prophet, of the exemplary as well as the emissary prophet and savior (Weber, *Rejections*, p. 327).[2]

For this reason, the natural allies of the prophets are the laity, as their natural foes are the priesthood of the communal temple. Yet, irrespective of the initial hostility between the priests and the prophets, they have, in occidental religions at any rate, collaborated in the cause of the ethical rationalization of the religious sphere. In this sense the message of the prophets of Western religions has been the polar opposite of that of magicians, who in a genetic and functional sense are held to be close relatives of prophecy. "Prophets and priests are the twin bearers of the systematization and rationalization of religious ethics" (Weber, *Economy I*, p. 439). In the process of substantive routinization of the content of the prophetic revelations, the priests often compromise the unity of the original message and the rigor of its "ethics of ultimate ends" (Weber, *Economy I*, pp.460, 465–466). In China, the communal religions (the cult of the state and the ancestors' cults), while preventing the satisfaction of the individual's quest for a mystic or ascetic salvation, tolerated the recourse of the masses to magic as long as the magicians kept their claims moderate and did not boast of being mystagogues or prophets (Weber, *China*, pp. 177–178, 200).

The uneducated masses do not usually find the intellectual and the virtuoso religious promises palatable. Thus, Weber assumed that all types of mass religiosity rest on similar forms of religious experience. A transcendental god, an impersonal cosmic order, or attainment of a state of bliss in a *nirvana* do not appeal to the religious tastes of the masses of peasantry and urban lower classes. This aversion to abstract religion is in part the result of the economic situation of these groups: without the necessary personal resources or leisure, they lack means to achieve such transcendental states of awareness. Furthermore, such abstract conceptions are not responsive to their own needs for a tangible emotional experience of the sacred and for emergency support when in distress. These primarily psychological needs have been behind the ubiquitous disinclination of the masses toward those rational concepts that characterize all soteriologies propounded by the intellectual strata (Weber, *India*, p. 236).

Weber was not too circumspect about venturing generalizations about religious needs of social classes. He suggested that a universal propensity for magic, idolatry, hagiolatry, and savior worship characterizes all mass religions of the world, and that they hold in common an interest in a semirational "theodicy" of suffering that has often taken the form of need for a just compensation in the hereafter (Weber, *Economy I*, p. 492). Also the interest in direct (often emotional or sensual) and noncontemplative experience of the holy has universally existed and led to mass popularity of orgiasticism, which was originally an exclusive trait of peasant religions (Weber, *Social*, p. 283).

Religions born among other social strata, as well as the great prophetic movements of the "occidental religions," have come into conflict with the religious tendencies of the masses. Sometimes the world religions have been able to temper, rationalize, or in rare cases, even eliminate certain religious beliefs of the masses. As a rule, however, the intellectualistic or prophetic religions themselves are liable to undergo drastic modifications to accommodate those lay groups that are not particularly or professionally concerned with the cultivation of intellectualism. Such changes of character are inevitable, especially when a religion of intellectuals is to be introduced to negatively privileged strata to whom contemplative religiosity is both economically and socially inaccessible (Weber, *Economy I*, p. 487).

The originally intellectualist Buddhism adopted *Tantrism* and *mantrism* as the most usable sources of ritualism for the consumption of the masses. Shivaist Brahmanhood achieved the same goal by incorporating phallic and apotropaic ecstasy and magic (Weber, *India*, p. 302). Also the transformation of the impersonal "Brahma" into a personal deity in orthodox Hinduism was a concession to lay needs (Weber, *India*, p. 173). To keep both the intellectual and lay groups interested and content, some religions have developed a rigorous dual organization of the laity and the ascetic or mystic virtuosi, and designated separate ethical obligations for them (Weber, *Economy I*, pp. 505, 506). Success in this linkage is a matter of survival for an originally elitist religion, as the alternative fates of successful Jainism and defeated Buddhism in India have so clearly demonstrated (Weber, *India*, pp, 196, 233, 291).

Besides incorporating elements of mass religiosity and organizing the laity, the intellectualistic religions have occasionally opted to live side by side with religious heterodoxies that are favored by the masses. As indicated earlier, the Confucian state cult allowed the plebeian Taoist priests and Buddhist monks to continue to cater to the needs of the masses (Weber, *China*, p. 201; *India*, p. 327). In Weber's view, this paralleled the toleration of philosophical metaphysics by the Hellenistic popular religion. In the latter case the state demanded only that the "subjects" observe their cultic duties in order to ward off collective misfortune, while the philosophers were allowed to elaborate on the duties of the "citizens" (Weber, *China*, pp. 175, 176).

The religious needs of the masses are characterized by Weber in yet another language, that of Feuerbach and Nietzsche: "What they [the underprivileged] cannot claim to be, they replace by the worth of what they will one day become." Weber, however, pushed this argument further. As the negatively privileged and the oppressed need psychological comfort in the face of "unequal distribution of good and bad luck," so do the privileged. It is not only for the sake of expediency that the privileged strata and classes have religious pretensions. As a rule, the fortunate one is not content with the fact that he is happy; he desires a "right" to his happiness, and will be inclined to embrace any ideology that assures him that he deserves what he has (Weber, *Economy I*, p. 491).

Religion for the Masses

Whatever its psychological value for various strata, religion has always been a concrete political force in history. One of its functions, as seen by both Marx and Weber, is its tranquilizing effect, allowing it to be used for the purposes of political domination.

The subjugated masses of conquered lands were frequently subjected to this kind of manipulation. "[It] was . . . the quite consistently pursued policy of the Persian kings, always to place the priesthood in the saddle as a useful tool for taming the dependent peoples." Weber considered it "objectively possible" that a Persian victory in Marathon would change the history of the Hellenistic and ultimately occidental civilizations by offering the Delphic and Orphic priests and prophets positions comparable to those held by the Babylonian and Israelite priesthoods under Persian kings from Cyrus to Artaxerxes (Weber, *Economy I*, pp. 454–455; *Judaism*, pp. 348–349). Evidence suggested to Weber that the priesthoods that serve a political function under great empires generally flourish after the annihilation of those political entities, should the conquerors choose to use the priests as instruments of pacifying the subjugated masses. The Islamic conquest of India brought about the demise of the prestigious ruling warrior caste (Kshatriya) while sustaining the most revered, but not necessarily powerful, priestly caste (Brahman) as instruments of social control (Weber, *India*, p. 125).

Religion as an "opium for the people" has also been used in domestic politics as a means of controlling the masses. The case of China is a good example of the legitimizing and thus stabilizing effect of religious ideas. The Confucian literati of China, aside from cultivating the notion of filial piety as a basis for legitimizing the political order, also passively tolerated certain elements of mass religiosity because it "guaranteed the docility of the masses" (Weber, *China*, p. 164). In Japan, "Buddhism was imported from India as a means of . . . taming the masses," a policy that apparently continued into the present century (Weber, *China*, p. 195; *India*, p. 271).

In India, the pacifying character of Hinduism was one of the most important reasons for its successful reception by Indian tribes. Notwithstanding the relatively inferior positions given to these communities, Hinduism perpetuated the dominance of the ruling strata within these tribes and therefore was naturally favored by all those who had a stake in preserving and perpetuating the socioeconomic status quo (Weber, *India*, p. 16).

During the restoration of Hinduism, its legitimizing aspects also played a decisive role in defeating Jainist and especially Buddhist heterodoxies. It was perceived as "an irresistible social force" that "could provide an incomparable religious support for the legitimation interest of the ruling strata" (Weber, *India*, p. 18).

Although occidental religions were of an entirely different caste and their relation to the structure of domination was at variance with those of Eastern religions, examples of manipulation of religion for political ends are by no means scarce in the West. In the Byzantine Empire, "Secular authorities were interested in using the monks as a means of domesticating the masses" (Weber, *India*, p. 245). The politically motivated tolerance toward mass religiosity (*Volksreligiosität*) by the dominant groups is best exemplified in the contemptuous indifference of the bureaucratic officials of all times toward the magical, emotional and irrational expressions of the religiosity of the masses (Weber, *Economy I*, pp. 476–477).

In a passionate passage Weber returns to this subject while discussing the attitude of the modern "privileged strata" whose scornful indifference to religious practices does not preclude their participation in the formal rituals of it. Yet the possibility of the emergence of a new congregational religion by or among them is considerably lessened because they are intent to preserve their social distance from the masses. The elite's abhorrence of mass enlightenment as a potential threat to their prestige is anchored in "the possibility that some new creed acceptable to large segments of the population could supplant the traditional creeds (from the texts of which everyone interprets something away, orthodoxy ten percent and liberals ninety percent)" (Weber, *Economy I*, pp. 516–517).

Examples such as these, scattered throughout Weber's substantive work on the world religions, support a Leninist sociology of religion, but are only one facet of Weber's theory of religion. While allowing for both categories of "religion of the masses" and "religion for the masses," Weber consistently opposed the reduction of the religious phenomena to either the psychological needs of the masses or the ideologies of the ruling classes.

Weber was equally averse to the glorification of religion as the revolutionary ideology of the oppressed masses. But he admitted first, that the prophetic religions have often formed a "protectorate of the weak," benefiting the socially downtrodden groups and strata (Weber, *Economy I*, p. 582). Second, he announced that although the prophets almost never directly descended from or represented the depressed classes, "in the great majority of cases, a prophetically announced religion of redemption has had its permanent locus among the less-favored social strata" (Weber, *Social*, p. 274). Finally, he pointed out that the practical ramifications of certain religious doctrines, such as the Buddhist indifference toward caste ritual, has benefited the lower echelons of the society (Weber, *India*, pp. 240, 256).

Weber perceived a variety of religious needs among the masses of peasantry and proletariat, as well as among the warriors, the civic and bureaucratic strata, and the intellectuals. Given the central role intellectuals have played in the development and incorporation of these needs into the body of religious literature, we shall focus on the various tensions and compromises that have linked the religiosity of these strata to the theoretical predilections and ideological manipulations of intellectuals.

Religion of the Warriors

Warriors and the masses have in common an aversion to the abstract theoretical conceptions of intellectuals. For instance, it is characteristic of heroic religions that instead of belief in "providence," "predestination," or in regarding salvation as a gift of grace bestowed by a transcendental and omnipotent god, such religions have gravitated toward the idea of irrational "fate" and "destiny," which is said to govern human beings and divinities alike (Weber, *Social*, p. 283; *Economy I*, p. 572). This opposition is best exemplified in the aforementioned mythological conflict between the passionate hero-god Indra and Varuna, the omniscient functional god of eternal order (Weber, *India*, p. 27).

The idea of an impersonal cosmic and social order found either in the intellectuals' speculative religions (such as Chinese "Tao" and Hindu "Rita") or the bureaucratic metaphysics of the intelligentsia (e.g., Confucian "Li") could not bring solace to the turbulent world of the warriors (Weber, *Economy I*, p. 431). The basic psychological experience for the warrior, Weber emphasized, is as a matter of course to face death and the irrationality of human destiny.

> Indeed, the chances and adventures of mundane existence fill his life to such an extent that he does not require of his religion (and accepts only reluctantly) anything beyond protection against evil magic or ceremonial rites congruent with his sense of status, such as priestly prayers for victory or for a blissful death leading directly into the hero's heaven. (Weber, *Economy I*, pp. 472–473)

The warriors also need to know that the god whom they implore is different from that of their enemy. Their next best alternative to overt polytheism is therefore monolatry (the exclusive worship of one of several deities) or henotheism (flattering only one god in order to solicit his favor). The martial hero might even demand that his god be physically present at the battlefield (Weber, *Judaism*, p. 133). Unlike the priestly and bureaucratic intelligentsia, warriors do not seek to legitimize their victory as a divine compensation for their piety. As they tend to regard their gods "as beings to whom envy is not unknown," their heroic feats are often accomplished despite their gods not because of them (Weber, *Economy I*, pp. 491–492). This characteristic of heroic religiosity sets it apart from both mass and intellectual religions.

In regard to their need for a tangible god that responds to the particular plight of the individual, the warriors' religion overlaps the religiosity of the masses; their heroic sense of pride leads away from the humility of the masses and from plebeian concepts such as sin and salvation (Weber, *Economy I*, p. 472).

With the nobility and the bureaucratic elite, warriors share a sense of superiority to, or at least are in competition with, the priestly circles and therefore do not easily genuflect before the prophet or priest (Weber, *Economy I*, p. 472). Thus the higher echelons of knightly orders in ancient India felt at ease with a proud denial of any form of belief in god espoused by Samkhya philosophy (Weber, *India*, p. 176). The consolidation of the caste system in India and the organic division of labor between priest and warrior castes were less than ideal for the latter, as the caste duties (*dharma*) of warriors did not allow them to transcend the monotony of everyday life through meditation and other esoteric means. The warriors' unwillingness to accept an inferior status generated a tension that was conducive to the creation of heterodox salvation religions in India (Weber, *India*, p. 181). This tension has everywhere generated an opposition against the monopoly of the priesthood over the sources of knowledge. In the cases of Indian Kshatriya and Japanese court knighthood, warriors have also emerged as a stratum of independent, literally schooled warrior-intellectuals (Weber, *India*, p. 333).

In an essay dealing with the more general aspects of the theory of religion ("Religious Rejections of the World and their Directions"), Weber went beyond elaborating on the distinctive religious needs of warriors and their ideological struggle against the religious ideas propounded by priestly groups. Weber argued that war makes for an unconditionally devoted community among the combatants and thus "releases an active mass compassion and love" for those involved. Their feelings tend to break down all the naturally given barriers of association and foster a brotherliness of war that competes with the brotherliness of the religious community (Weber, *Rejections*, pp. 335–336). Religions have responded to this challenge, above all, by rejecting the worldly pride of the hero (Weber, *Social*, p. 291). Yet Weber believed that the religions can offer only two consistent solutions for this problem: (1) a mystic world flight, which implies a radical antipolitical attitude and seeks an acosmic and benevolent brotherliness, or (2) a puritan inner-worldly ascetic solution setting out to impose God's revealed commandments upon the world, without excluding the use of violence.

Finally, reference must be made to a classification of religions that Weber developed by associating world religions with the specific ethos of the leading strata that emerged as their major bearers: "as a rule one may determine the strata whose styles of life have been at least predominantly decisive for certain religions" (Weber, *Social*, pp. 268, 269). In *Economy and Society* he sums it up thus:

> If one wishes to characterize succinctly, in a formula so to speak, the types representative of the various strata that were the primary carriers or propagators of the so-called world religions, they would be following: In Confucianism, the world-organizing bureaucrat; in Hinduism, the world ordering magician; in Buddhism, the mendicant monk wandering through the world; in Islam, the warrior seeking to conquer the world; in Judaism, the wandering trader; and in Christianity, the itinerant journeyman. (Weber, *Economy I*, p. 512)

Although this classification is clearly consistent with the premises of his sociology of knowledge, Weber once more emphasizes that

> all these types must not be taken as exponents of their own occupational or material "class interests," but rather as the ideological carriers of the kind of ethical or salvation doctrine which rather readily conformed to their social position. (Weber, *Economy I*, p. 512)

The point of contention, however, is an empirical not a methodological one. An empirically plausible case may well be made against Weber's claim that Islam was the religion of "world conquering warriors," or "a knight order of disciplined crusaders" (Weber, *Social*, p. 269). Here, we shall refrain from launching such an extensive project. However, a brief argument on the inconsistency of this assertion with Weber's own quasi-general laws concerning the elective affinities between religious doctrines and the ideological needs of the warriors will be presented in Appendix C.

Religion of the Civic Strata

Max Weber's generalizing observations about elective affinities between the ideal interests of social strata and the content of their religiosity are least conclusive in the case of plebeian or civic groups, that is, those city dwellers who neither share in political power of a military or corvée state nor belong to the influential nobility of the cities (Weber, *Judaism*, p. 224). The civic petite-bourgeoisie and artisan groups seem to have generally gravitated toward a variety of diverse, even contrasting religious concepts.

These have included caste taboos and magical or mystagogic religions of both the sacramental or orgiastic types in India, animism in China, dervish religion in Islam, and pneumatic enthusiastic congregational religion of early Christianity, practiced particularly in the eastern half of the Roman Empire. Still other modes of religious expression among these groups are *deisidaimonia* as well as orgiastic worship of Dionysos in ancient Greece, Pharisaic fidelity to the law in ancient urban Judaism, an essentially idolatrous Christianity as well as all sorts of sectarian faiths in the Middle Ages, and various types of Protestantism in early modern times. (Weber, *Economy I*, p. 481)

These striking disparities led Weber to reassert the main premise of his sociology of knowledge concerning the autonomy of the sphere of ideas. It was obvious that various forms of traditional capitalism had not automatically produced uniform ethical or religious forms. Yet he suggested that "an affinity between economic rationalism and certain types of rigoristic ethical religion" may have always existed (Weber, *Economy I*, p. 480). But Weber did not characterize the nature of this affinity in terms of class ideologies; instead, he explained it in a way that conforms to our earlier description of "reverse determination": once a religion that is potentially conducive to the needs of the civic strata emerges, it can easily win followers among various ranks of plebeians (Weber, *Economy I*, p. 484). In his most misunderstood book, *The Protestant Ethic and the Spirit of Capitalism*, Weber attempted to underline exactly this point. The intellectually autonomous yet historically consequential break with Christian theology introduced by Reformation thinkers facilitated the uniting of the ideal and material interests of the occidental bourgeoisie in the form of Protestant work ethics, providing a crucial impetus for the emergence of modern capitalism. The latter developments, which had been an "objective possibility" at the time of the disintegration of feudalism in the West, was "adequately caused"[3] by favorable economic and cultural situations. Weber's comparative studies demonstrated that capitalism may otherwise have remained dormant in Europe, as it did elsewhere, and that the introduction of the Reformation and its enthusiastic reception by the Christian civic strata played an indispensable role in this most decisive of the social changes in the Occident.

The occidental path toward capitalism was also already paved by the successful eradication of magic that was achieved by the Israelite prophets. Abandonment of the rural way of life and settlement in the cities seem to have universally encouraged the process of "demagification," as the need for magical manipulation of nature was progressively replaced by a need for ethically rational regulation of urban life. Yet a total demagification of the religious realm was thoroughly consummated only in the West (Weber, *Social*, p. 284). Similarly, in general, the weakening of the blood groupings and clans in urban settings could have set the stage for the emergence of congregational religions as well as occupational guild organizations. But these characteristic civic developments were not to appear in Chinese or Indian civilizations, as they were thwarted by the lingering significance of ancestral cult and clan exogamy in the former and the rigor of religious caste taboos in the latter (Weber, *Economy I*, p. 482).

These "exceptions" to the "rule" are far too significant to be discarded as anomalies or even "exceptions." It is only in view of Weber's value-relevant interest in Western capitalism that they appear so. Besides, Weber wished to demonstrate that the universal penchant of the civic strata for an ethically rationalized religion remained ascendant by contrasting the religions of the civic strata to those of the peasantry and the military. For instance, the need for calculability and instrumental rationality can be perceived in the inclination of civic strata toward a compensatory religious mechanism (Weber, *Economy I*, p. 483). The peasants, like the warriors, were resistant to this concept; it loomed too remote for the former and too trite for the latter. Conversely, the violent and heroic mythologies of the warrior-gods could not soothe the sentimental and edifying inwardness of the urban strata. Thus the emergence of the bourgeoisie has everywhere changed the focus of the secondary sources of religious literature:

> This middle-class transformation of religion in the direction of domesticity is illustrated by the emergence of the god-suffused *bhakti* piety in all Hindu cults, both in the creation of the Bodhisattva figure as well as in the cults of Krishna; and by the popularity of the edifying myths of the child Dionysos, Osiris, the Christ child, and their numerous parallels. (Weber, *Economy I*, p. 488)

The need of the urban strata for a compensatory system has compelled even the most uncompromisingly intellectualistic religions to introduce changes in their promises of salvation. Thus as the Buddhist contemplative mendicant monk desired to enter *nirvana* (a state that in the ancient texts is identified with absolute annihilation), the laity were allowed to seek compensation in the hereafter and to develop what Weber called "an extremely colorless 'bourgeois' ethic," which aimed at attaining present rewards of riches and worldly fame (Weber, *India*, pp. 215, 228). Buddhism, however, was originally attractive to the urban laity, as it held the promise of liberation from the rigid Hindu social bonds, namely, that of restricting education to the highest caste (Weber, *India*, pp. 240, 256).

Although Confucianism stands out as the quintessential exemplification of the bureaucratic religion, or rather irreligion, its sober and optimistic rationalism, its inner-worldly morality, and its emphasis on the cosmic and social order seem to have also engrossed the attention of lay and civic groups (Weber, *Economy I*, p. 476). As a religion of bureaucratic intelligentsia and genteel literati, however, it scorned the common man's search for this worldly or other worldly theodicies and developed in the direction of an esoteric belief in an unfathomable providence (Weber, *China*, pp. 152–153, 206–207). Thus, Confucian sage bureaucrats shared the Jewish belief that only the fulfillment of the commandments of heaven can safeguard the destiny of the state. The similarity, however, is merely incidental, as the social carriers of Judaism were not aesthetically cultured literati but plebeian intelligentsia who emerged as the exponents of a rational religious ethic (Weber, *Judaism*, p. 224).

The beginnings of a similar plebistic religiosity can also be detected in ancient Egypt and Babylon, where further rationalization and systematization of the workaday ethic was prevented by the persistence of magic. The continued significance of magical practices in these civilizations can be explained by the fact that they served the material interests of the respective priesthoods, who not only tolerated but also systematized and developed magic (Weber, *Judaism*, pp. 222, 249). In contrast, the substantive message of the Israelite prophecy made it impossible for the priesthood to pander to the religious demands of the masses. Instead, by advocating a puritanical, antiorgiastic, anti-idolatrous, and antimagical religiosity, they altered the countenance of occidental religiosity decisively and permanently (Weber, *Judaism*, pp. 223-224). The rabbinical priesthood, which was the main instrument of this opposition and represented institutionalized Judaism, was profoundly civic and plebistic; most of the personalities recognized in the Talmud were neither poor nor predominantly wealthy but gainfully employed artisans (Weber, *Judaism*, pp. 393-394). As a stratum of plebeian intellectuals, "the rabbis rejected asceticism as well as the intellectual mysticism of a salvation aristocracy" (Weber, *Judaism*, pp. 392-400). The contrast of Judaism to the Chinese case is especially striking because the plebeian intelligentsia in China produced a class of priest-magicians who in the guise of Taoist heterodoxy indulged the mass interest in subjects such as achieving longevity and ultimately rationalized and systematically incorporated popular magic into the originally intellectualist Taoism (Weber, *China*, pp. 199-201) .

The discussion of plebeian intellectuality indicates that Weber did not restrict intellectual manipulation of symbols to the socially and economically privileged groups. It also shows that the diversity of cultural ideas and their autonomy from the sphere of material interests renders any strict economically deterministic interpretation of ideologies impossible. A thorough comparative study of Chinese and Judaic plebeian intellectuals could provide a convincing case for the limits of abstract class analysis of religious ideologies. Of course, as we descend into the lower layers of the civic strata, the correspondence between ideas and interests becomes more evident.

The quasi-proletarian intellectualism of the lowest urban strata and that of the self-taught peasant groups display a radical originality in contemplating the meanings of the cosmos, social conventions, and religious dogma. Weber observed that the intensity of the "pariah intellectualism" of those groups that comprise the lower rungs of the social hierarchy is due to the fact that they "stand to a certain extent on the point of Archimedes in relation to social conventions, both in respect to the external order and in respect to common opinions" (Weber, *Economy I*, p. 507). Relative freedom from the bounds of social conventions and material considerations accounts for the originality and emotional intensity of their religious experiences. In his *Ancient Judaism* Weber offers an interesting parallel to this line of reasoning. In that study, instead of being in the lowest strata of the society, the denizens of the geographical margins of a dominant culture occupy the point of Archimedes:

> Rarely have entirely new religious conceptions originated in the respective centers of rational cultures. Rational prophetic or reformist innovations were first conceived, not in Babylon, Athens, Alexandria, Rome, Paris, London, Cologne, Hamburg, Vienna, but in Jerusalem of pre-exilic, Galilaea of late Jewish times, in the late Roman province of Africa, in Assisi, in Wittenberg, Zurich, Geneva and in the marginal regions of the Dutch, lower-German, and English cultural areas, like Frisia and New England. To be sure this never occurred without the influence of a neighboring rational civilization. The reason for this is always the same: prerequisite to new religious conceptions is that man must not yet have unlearned how to face the course of the world with questions of his own. Precisely the man distant from the great culture centers has cause to do so when their influence begins to affect or threaten his central interests. Man living in the midst of the culturally satiated areas and enmeshed in their technique addresses such questions just as little to the environment as, for instance, the child used to daily tramway rides would chance to question how the tramway actually manages to start moving.
>
> The possibility of questioning the meaning of the world presupposes the capacity to be astonished about the course of events. (Weber, *Judaism*, pp. 206–207)

Between the "proletariod" and the middle civic strata one finds an intellectualism representing the ideal interests of the journeymen. On the one hand, they were influenced by the ethically rational religiosity of the petite bourgeoisie, for they aspired to join them by eventually setting up their own shop. On the other, their constant teetering on the edges of the minimum subsistence, "their workaday deprivations, the fluctuations in the price of their daily bread, their job insecurity and their dependence on fraternal assistance" made them more receptive to the unofficial heterodoxies (Weber, *Economy I*, pp. 484–486). Christianity, Weber argued, was originally a religion of itinerant journeymen and artisans with strong petite bourgeoisie and civic leanings (Weber, *Economy I*, pp. 462, 512; *Social*, p. 269).

Religion of the Intellectuals

As mentioned before, Weber's numerous allusions to the intellectuality of the warriors, the petite bourgeoisie, the journeymen, and the proletariat indicate that he did not confine the production of rational (practical or theoretical) concepts to any particular stratum or class. Indeed, the sociology of intellectuals can give full reign to speculative generalizations concerning the correspondence of ideas and interests, only when studying the intellectuality of nonintellectual strata. In these cases the elective affinities between ideas and interests are more clearly delineated. This correspondence, however, becomes obscured in the case of intellectuals as they produce "ideas" that do not necessarily reinforce their material or even ideal interests. To cope with this problem, Weber based his sociology of intellectuals on a delicate balance of two theoretical assumptions. First, he postulated the "relative autonomy" of the sphere of ideas from socioeconomic forces. Second, Weber proceeded with a theory of historical causation that we have dubbed "reverse determination," whereby the interest is shifted from the origin to the popularization of a religion according to the ideal and material interest of various strata and classes. The relative significance of these assumptions varies according to the level of analysis and the empirical characteristics of the particular form of intellectuality under investigation.

While, for Weber, intellectuals may comprise a separate stratum or class with its own particular ideal and material interests, the assumption of the relative autonomy of the sphere of ideas prohibits the categorical attribution of an ideological character to all of the thought products of an intellectual stratum. Intellectuals, as producers of ideas and makers of ideologies, both for themselves and other strata and classes, cannot be understood in terms of a monolithic (emanationist or materialistic) theory of knowledge. An emanationist theory would be unable to account for either the ideological dimension of human thought or for its historically determined character. A materialistic sociology of knowledge, on the other extreme, is also unable to proceed with a consistent class analysis of ideas produced by intellectual strata. How can such an approach account for a very common phenomenon: the producers of ideas that are inimical to the ideologies of the intellectual class, or the class which patronizes them, are also intellectuals. The chilling effect of this irony on theories not equipped with the proper intellectual apparatus to deal with it is evident in the history of Marxist thought. Even those Marxist theorists who realized this dilemma and tried to come to grips with it treated it as a mere practical question of party politics and stopped short of integrating the solution into their theoretical perspective (Lenin, 1973). Besides, in the sphere of religious ideas it is a very common phenomenon that the proponents of both sides of an orthodox–heterodox controversy belong to the same class or stratum of intellectuals (Weber, *China*, pp. 183–185; *India*, pp. 192–193; *Judaism*, pp. 167–168).

According to Weber, although intellectuals do in most instances constitute a separate stratum, they do not necessarily pursue their status "interests" in their own intellectual contemplations. This leaves only intellectuals, not workers (and even some Marxist theorists agree on this with Weber), able to transcend their class interests because they are the bearers of various forms and levels of "rationality" (mainly substantive-theoretical rationality), which follow their own relatively autonomous developmental rules (Kolakowski, 1968, p. 159).[4]

We have in the course of this chapter alluded to the fact that intellectuals have felt a profound disdain for irrational elements of mass religiosity such as orgiasticism, mortificatory practices, and magic. Whether this attitude has been translated into active opposition to, reconstruction and rationalization of, or a distant calculated tolerance toward such elements is a matter of individual civilizational diversities.

Generally speaking, however, intellectuals have always been the exponents of theoretical rationalism (Weber, *Social*, p, 279).[5] It is this aspect of the ideal interests of intellectuals, not their narrower material interests, which has had the most lasting effect on the development of religious thought (Weber, *Rejections*, p. 352). The penchant of intellectuals for theoretical rationality is even more pronounced when contrasted to the practical rationality of the civic strata, which is geared to the solution of everyday practical needs. Although the two types of rationality are both generically and historically related, they have had very diverse influences upon the development of religious ideas. There is, for instance, an elective affinity between otherworldly mysticism or a desire to be the vessel of the divine and the intellectuals' quest for salvation. Conversely, the inner-worldly ascetic desire to be conceived as the "instrument of a god" in the world has resonated with the practical needs of civic strata (Weber, *Social*, pp. 285, 286).

The effects of intellectualization on the economic ethics of the world religions have been profound and heterogeneous. For instance, instead of steering masses toward a methodical way of life (as had happened in the occidental religions) the intellectualistic religions of India have condoned and benefited from the economic irrationality in regard to accumulation of property and the evaluation of capital (Weber, *India*, p. 328). As a rule, within the sphere of religion, intellectuals have universally strived to attain a meaningful picture of the world precisely because they experienced it as senseless "thus, the demand has been implied: that the world order in its totality is, could, and somehow should be a meaningful 'cosmos.' This quest, the core of genuine religious rationalism, has been borne precisely by strata of intellectuals" (Weber, *Social*, p. 281). The creation of a well-organized pantheon of gods, like the appearance of rationalized magic, is indicative of the presence of systematic thinking and ultimately of an intellectual effort toward theoretical or at least formal rationality (Weber, *Economy I*, p. 407; *India*, p. 152). Thus, the religions of intellectuals, when unable to promote transcendental monotheism, tend to exult the heavenly gods and the lords of the stars whose course is regulated and fixed forever (Weber, *Judaism*, p. 153; *Economy I*, p. 410). The intellectuals have naturally welcomed those world religions that promote the idea of an absolutely transcendental, omnipotent, and omniscient god (Weber, *Economy I*, pp. 419, 518).[6]

Weber repeatedly emphasized that the prerequisite for the acceptance of intellectuals in organized religions is a "sacrifice of the intellect" (Weber, *Economy I*, p. 567; *Science*, p. 154; *Rejections*, p. 351). The implication is that a universal skepticism is also characteristic of the intellectuals, which he pronounces more explicitly in another context: "The skeptical point of view has been common to the intellectual strata of every period. It is evident in the Greek epitaphs and in the highest artistic productions of the Renaissance, such as the works of Shakespeare; it has found expression in the philosophies of Europe, China, and India, as well as in modern intellectualism" (Weber, *Economy I*, p. 568).[7]

Having touched upon some characteristic inclinations evinced in the religions of intellectuals, we will now turn to the role of intellectuals in the development of the world's religions.

Intellectuals and the World Religions

A set of ideas that has an elective affinity with, or is responsive to, the needs of intellectuals is likely to be consolidated into a religion of intellectuals. Such a development has been actualized to varying degrees only in the religions of India and China, but its nuclei can also be found in occidental religions. Even when fully realized (as in the case of ancient Buddhism), religions of intellectuals have had to come into contact with other types of religiosity. Tensions and compromises that have resulted from these contacts are depicted throughout Weber's sociology of religion.

The fact that Weber referred to occidental religions as "plebeian" not "intellectualistic," as he called Indian and to some extent Chinese religions, does not mean that in his view intellectuals had nothing to do with the development of Judaism and Christianity. On the contrary, their anti-intellectualism, as elsewhere, is usually connected to intellectuals. The tendency toward theoretical rationalization of the religious sphere, for example, is evident in the development of these religions (Weber, *Rejections*, p. 351). The increasing consistency with which idolatry is condemned and monism is promoted in the Old Testament, as well as the texture of certain postexilic sections of it (namely, Deuteronomy), illustrates a "theological zeal for consistency" that is characteristic of intellectualism (Weber, *Judaism*, p. 70). Furthermore, the fundamental change of Yahweh from a war god or a master of rainfall into "a wise governor of the Universe," not to mention the belief in divine providence, could not have been developed without the presence of intellectuals and their ideal interests in the process of intellectual rationalization (Weber, *Judaism*, pp. 129, 311).

But Judaism never became a religion of intellectuals because of the decisive presence of its unique phenomenon of prophecy. Jewish prophecy exemplifies the autonomy of the sphere of ideas, as its nature cannot be explained by an analysis of the ideologies of intellectuals or any other social group. Prophets waged war against and successfully obliterated the intellectuality of royal courts (i.e., the prophecy of good fortune) and subjugated the plebeian intellectuality of the priests. This prevented a total monopolization of the culture by the intellectualist strata, which had happened in India. Jewish prophecy also killed the embryo of court intellectuality, which could have developed into a Confucian-type cult of the state.

Christianity carried the anti-intellectualism of the Jewish prophets to its extreme. Jesus, like other Jewish prophets, clashed with the plebeian intellectualism of the Pharisees. Christianity is a "non-intellectual's proclamation directed to non-intellectuals, to the 'poor in spirit'" (Weber, *Economy I*, p. 631). The early Christian church followed suit by suppressing autonomous intellectualistic movements, namely, Gnosticism. This battle was continued by priestly intelligentsia who, through proclaiming "dogmas," restrained the irresponsibility of pure intellectualism (Weber, *Economy I*, pp. 462–63).

The same anti-intellectualistic power of prophecy also achieved unparalleled victories in curbing the central tendencies of occidental mass religiosity. The orgiastic worship of agricultural deities (known under the term *Baal*) was strictly condemned by the Old Testament (Weber, *Judaism*, p. 189). Judaism and then Christianity fought against magic with considerable success. However, the history of Judeo-Christian opposition to mass religiosity is not entirely devoid of compromises. To mention only one example: certain modified versions of hagiolatry as well as savior worship have been tolerated by the Catholic church.

Nevertheless, the fundamental anti-intellectualistic attitude of Christianity remained unchanged. The belief survives still that "the intellectual mastery of the world leads away from god, not toward him," for the charisma of faith was granted by God to children and minors rather than to scholars (Weber, *Economy I*, pp. 553, 568).

A striking contrast to the occidental religions is presented by the soteriology of Indian and Chinese intellectuals. Despite the differences in Indian and Chinese civilizations, there existed in both a status group composed of genteel literati whose charisma rested on knowledge. Both groups developed the same pride in education and a similar rationalism to fight the irrationality of mass religiosity (Weber, *India*, pp. 137, 139).

Ironically, these intellectualistic religions were less successful than the so-called "plebeian religions" in fighting the tendencies of mass religiosity. Intrinsically dependent and historically bound to magical charisma, the Indian Brahmanhood was unable to fight magic. Yet, an attempt was made, as it is expected of intellectuals to rationalize and sublimate the magical holy states (Weber, *India*, p. 152). The banning of certain extreme ecstatic and orgiastic semi-magical practices as well as the rationalization and modification of magically related mysticism are the results of this Brahmanical intellectual influence (Weber, *India*, pp. 148–149).

In his "Religious Rejections Of The World And Their Directions," Weber argued that because of an irreconcilable tension between the religious and intellectual spheres, all religions demand of religious intelligentsia an "intellectual sacrifice" that amounts to a limitation of their untempered rationalism (Weber, *Rejections*, p. 351). What happened in India, however, far exceeded this. In the process of reforming Hinduism, the Brahmanical priesthood, partly to compete with the Buddhist heterodoxy and partly because of its immediate material interests, populated the relatively empty pantheon of the Hindu religion with local demigods, agricultural deities, and deified saviors. Hagiolatry and deification of live or dead gurus as "saviors in need" were also introduced into modern Hinduism. The orgiastic ecstasy of Tantrism, however, had still to be greatly modified before finding its niche in later Hindu practices (Weber, *India*, p. 297). Both Shivaist and Vishnuist forms of later Hinduism are, thus, historical altars on which the most extravagant "sacrifice of intellect" has been performed (Weber, *India*, p. 309).

As Christianity carried the anti-intellectualistic tendencies of Judaism to the extreme, so Buddhism carried the original intellectualism of Hindu religion to its logical conclusion. "Buddhism is the most consistent of the salvation doctrines produced before and after by the intellectualism of educated Indian strata" (Weber, *Economy I*, p. 628). It behooved this "uncompromisingly consistent" soteriology of Hindu intellectuals to announce that neither greed nor lust but stupidity is the source of all evil (Weber, *India*, pp. 233, 252). Yet witness how Buddhism, by disregarding the religious needs of the masses, lost the battle to modern Hinduism and was reincarnated once again only when it became a "religion for the masses" in China and Japan and a "religion of the masses" in the forms of later Mahayana Buddhism and Lamaism. When it finally emerged in Japan as Zen Buddhism, it assumed the character of a "religion of warriors" (Weber, *India*, pp. 256, 270, 278). Its original intellectualistic quest for nirvana, its promise of absolute annihilation after death, as well as its proud renunciation of both world and deities, were eventually drastically modified, if not forgotten (Weber, *India*, p. 215).

In China, both orthodox Confucianism and heterodox Taoism were originally religions of the intellectuals. The former exemplified the bureaucratic indifference toward religious feelings, and the latter epitomized the escapism of ivory tower intellectuals (Weber, *China*, pp. 143–192). Confucian mandarins cultivated the inner-worldly morality of laymen and admonished the masses to adjust themselves to the imperial social system said to directly mirror the cosmic harmony. Not unlike other ideologies forged to legitimize patrimonial systems, Confucianism emphasized filial piety as the ultimate virtue and tried to extend its domain beyond the limits of family and class organizations to regulate also the relation of the masses to state officials and ultimately to the pontifex. While tolerating certain traits of mass religiosity, such as ancestor worship and magic, Confucian ethics despised and on occasions fought against Buddhist as well as Taoist individualistic escapism. It must be mentioned that Taoism also had to reach some kind of compromise with mass religiosity. This did not take the shape of rationalization of magic (as in Hinduism) or a mere distant toleration of it (as in Confucianism), but rather a coarse coexistence with, or at times a thorough incorporation of it (Weber, *China*, pp. 152–153, 191–192).

The characterization of ideal typical elective affinities between religious ideas and spiritual as well as material interests is more problematic in the case of the intellectual strata. This is due to two major causes. First, the substantive rationalization of the content of religion by the elite of a religious intelligentsia can produce unexpected ideological results, such as anticlerical or anti-intellectualistic ideologies dividing the ranks of consolidated intellectual strata or preventing such consolidation. Second, ideological chasms deepen between the ranks of intellectuals whenever some of them consciously ally themselves with other strata or classes promoting anti-intellectualism. Furthermore, the dissimilarity of the religious needs of the lay intellectuals and those of the clerical intelligentsia has contributed to the recurrent rise of heterodoxies as well as new anticlerical orthodoxies.

Religions, Intellectuals, and the Rationalization Paradox

Intellectuals have been the bearers of various levels and forms of rationality. As such, they have always been closer to the autonomous core of ideas that develop through intellectual contemplation. Besides producing relatively abstract ideas and concepts, they also play a role in the reinterpretation of ideas. They construct ideologies not only for themselves but also for the other strata and classes. We have already enlarged on the pivotal role the intellectuals have played in the systematization and rationalization of the "ethical religions" (Judaism under Persian kings, Buddhism in Japan, etc.). Yet intellectuals leave their imprint on mass religiosity in a variety of other ways as well.

In their search for the meaning of the universe, especially wherever the process of demagification has been completed, intellectuals have tried to fit the world into their rational schema (Weber, *Rejections*, p. 350). In doing so they have also imparted meaning to suffering, which otherwise would be experienced as unjust and meaningless. The formulation of theodicies is an intellectual by-product for which there is a great demand, especially among the masses. Of course, intellectuals too have a need for theodicy because, both as individuals and members of a distinct status group, they also experience the unequal distribution of good and bad fortune (Weber, *Social*, p. 275). But they do more than provide for a rational understanding of their own plight. They also give clues for deciphering the "meaning" of the suffering of the other strata and classes. All theodicies are first shared only by intellectual strata (Weber, *Judaism*, p. 305). This is usually not a service but an "unintended consequence" of intellectual activity of the cultured strata. But no matter who eventually benefits from the various cultural products of intellectuals, the fact remains that they are the carriers of a rationalism that itself is not determined by the material or ideal interests of any stratum, including their own. By suggesting this, Weber rejected all theories of the materialistic as well as psychologistic determination of ideas without denying the influence that such "interests" might exert on the process of reinterpretation of ideas and the creation of "ideologies."

Although later Buddhism catered to the psychological and emotional needs of the masses as well as to the material needs of tyrannical rulers before finally turning into the gospel of "discipline-seeking warriors," its intellectualism originally addressed "the metaphysical needs of the human mind as it is driven to reflect on ethical and religious questions, driven not by material need but by an inner compulsion to understand the world as a meaningful cosmos and take up a position toward it" (Weber, *Economy I*, p. 499).[8]

To take this discussion beyond the sphere of sociology and the study of the interplay of ideas and interests, let us suggest that there is still another source of tension: the fundamental incongruity between the rationalizing processes and the ontologically unrationalizable "nature" of the world. Intellectuals, Weber argues, expose the religious interpretation of the world to the imperative of consistency and attempt to systematize and rationalize religious ethics (Weber, *Rejections*, p. 324; *Economy I*, p. 439). But the "world" as seen by Weber undermines them all by either refusing to fit entirely into these rational frameworks (we call this under-rationalization), or if it is pushed into such rationalistic pigeon-holes (we call this over-rationalization), it eventually rebels against them. In the latter case, the apparently successful rationalization of a world image is ridiculed, discarded, or both.

The closest metaphysics has come to capturing the truth of the Weberian world is when it surrenders to polytheism wherein the world is but the battlefield of warring gods (Weber, *Meaning*, p. 17). Those religions that have chosen to neglect the irreconcilability of life spheres by rejecting polytheism (as intellectuals tend to do) have had to deal with the frustrating refusal of the world to conform to their rationalistic demands. The result of this has been a tendency toward an ascetic or a mystic flight from the world (Weber, *Rejections*, pp. 332, 357).

But the disenchantment of the modern world makes a religious flight from the mundane world impossible. Intellectuals, in modern times, have had to confront the irrationality of a recalcitrant world without being able to resolve their dilemma by abnegating the worldly and searching for tranquility in a beyond or even in a worldly state of bliss. Modern intellectuals have not followed their forefathers, who, attempting to conceal the irrational cores of the world, wove endless layers of rationality around them. They have chosen instead to indulge in the irrational cores of life, refusing even to steer a course around them. This plunge into the irrational is encouraged by the reification of instrumental reason in post-Protestant industrialism. Intellectuals are the first to shudder at the touch of "the cold skeleton hands of rational orders" and to flee from "the banality of everyday routine" (Weber, *Rejections*, p. 347).

All these propositions, however, are based on a fundamental ontological position: that the world as it stands can never be thoroughly rationalized—"the calculation of consistent rationalism has not easily come out even with nothing left over" (Weber, *Social*, p. 281). The theoretical implications of this ontological postulation are far reaching. They led Weber beyond the sociological analysis of the process of reinterpretation of ideas in the context of ideal and material interests. In the philosophical frame against which Weber examines ideas, the ineradicable and eternal contradictions of the world appear almost everywhere. The world is obdurately irrational, and any attempt to subsume this paradoxical whole under an overreaching rational system or to introduce mathematical consistency into it is not only doomed to failure but further intensifies the existing contradictions by highlighting the otherwise hidden tensions in the mundane world (Weber, *Politics*, p. 123; *Rejections*, p. 357). In other words, the intellectual rationalizations of the world image, by drawing attention to the problems that they attempt to solve, defeat their purpose. They are likely to rob people of the only protective shield they wear against the disturbing influence of the contradictions of this world, namely their ignorance of them. The existence of irrational cores and the irreconcilability of the several life spheres result in a perpetual "under-rationalization" of the intellectuals' world image. But intellectuals have not been entirely unsuccessful in producing universalistic rational interpretations of the world. Certain eschatologies, for example, have created fairly consistent and meaningful interpretations of the world and of its evil and suffering. Yet, in Weber's view, the most perfect theodicies are often the most useless. The substantive rationalization of religious world images leads to the irrationalization of religious behavior as the practical rationalism aimed at this world recedes and the mundane world is rejected for its refusal to conform to the meaning that it is supposed to contain (Weber, *Economy I*, p. 424).

The most theoretically successful accounts justifying undeserved suffering are the doctrines of *karma*, dualism, and predestination. They can be characterized as rationally closed systems (Weber, *Rejections*, p. 358). Of the three, the dualism doctrine "is the most radical solution of the problem of theodicy, and for that very reason it provides as little satisfaction for ethical claims upon god as does the belief in predestination" (Weber, *Economy I*, p. 526). The same is true of the doctrine of *karma*. No matter how unambiguously it provides for an ethical rationalization of the world order, once the question of the meaning of this gigantic machine of compensation is raised, it can be experienced as "dreadful" (Weber, *India*, p. 132). A similar situation exists in the case of the so-called occidental religions: "The more the development tends toward the conception of a transcendental unitary god who is universal, the more there arises the problem of how the extraordinary power of such a god may be reconciled with the imperfection of the world that he has created" (Weber, *Economy I*, p. 519).

This process has fueled the search of the masses for their own easy solutions (e.g., mass religiosity) or for new, more responsive religions. To bring this point closer to home, take the example of Leibnitz's "the best of all possible worlds." While this idea was enunciated by others before him, once he attempted to bring everything together into a theologically closed system vindicating the goodness of God, the result became as "perfectly" irrational and as ludicrous as the world of Voltaire's *Candide*.

3

Max Weber's Sociology of Politics as a Sociology of Intellectuals

In this chapter we shall draw upon Max Weber's political sociology and his political writings only insofar as they shed light on the relationship between politics and intellectuality. Weber's futurology, that is, his assessment of the objective possibilities of occidental civilization and the trajectory of its future development, is also relevant to the purposes of this chapter. Insights Weber had gained in the course of his studies in the field of comparative historical sociology about the developmental trends of the Western world helped shape his political ideals and the strategies he favored for achieving them. As intellectuals and intelligentsia appear as two of the major protagonists in Weber's grand scenario about the future of the Occident, a brief taxonomical note on the differences of the ideal types of intellectuals and intelligentsia seems to be in order. Further elaboration of this topic, in accordance with the Weberian methodological tradition, has been deferred to the last chapter of this book.

When contrasted to intelligentsia—whom we define as the aggregate of the educated members of one particular stratum or some strata, possessing varying degrees of "status consciousness"—the category of intellectuals comprises a small group of highly creative (often individualistic) individuals. An often borrowed analogy from economics portrays intellectuals as "producers" of those intellectual goods that are later disseminated and "consumed" in the marketplace of ideal and material interests of the intelligentsia and (through their mediation) of other classes and strata. Another useful metaphor describes the function of intelligentsia in the process of dissemination of these ideas as a "transmission belt" that constantly and progressively remolds and simplifies the ideas produced by the leading intellectuals.

Relating to Ideologies: Intellectuals and Intelligentsia

We may accept the previous definition of the two categories, of intellectuals and intelligentsia, as consistent with Weberian concepts regarding the hierarchical classification of intellectuals and intelligentsia.[1] A more important distinction, however, can be perceived if we examine, from the Weberian point of view, the respective attitudes of intellectuals and intelligentsia toward the sphere of ideas: intelligentsia will be found more willing than intellectuals to view ideas instrumentally. The intelligentsia are better disposed to "hang on" to the solidified ideas (ideologies) that serve their interests.

By contrast, the intellectuals' attitude toward ideas is less determined by practical considerations. This is not meant to imply that intellectuals are more apt to disregard their own interests for the sake of ideas. Rather, it means that their "ideal interests" (in tracing the immanent process of rationalization) counterbalances, occasionally precedes, and may even contradict) their material interests. Practical consequences of ideas, therefore, even when they adversely affect intellectuals' material interests, cannot solely dictate the contents of intellectuals' beliefs and thoughts. The push and pull of ideal and material interests of intellectuals have greatly influenced the development of knowledge and the status of its carriers in a variety of civilizational contexts. Thus it is of cardinal importance to the sociologies of intellectuals and knowledge to appreciate the centrality of this immanent tension. Although the locus of this tension is not between the general spheres of ideas and interests— but in the balance of ideal and material interests of intellectuals—in explaining the nature of this built-in strain, we might use the paradigm of separate spheres of "ideas" and "interests" as a heuristic device.

Intellectuals may be thought of as carriers of the substantive and theoretical rationalization of ideas. If we assume, as Weber did, that the sphere of ideas is relatively autonomous from that of economics, then intellectuals as the sounding board of the sphere of ideas represent an anomaly: they do not necessarily advocate ideas that are conducive to their material interests. What has appeared to some philosophers of history as the teleological movement of ideas toward increasing logical consistency is indeed both mediated and fueled by intellectuals' ideal interests in imparting meaning to the world and perfecting such meanings. In any case, however, the logic of the development of ideas is independent from that of the material interests—of both intellectuals and other classes and strata.

The social consequences of indulging in the sphere of pure ideas for intellectuals are twofold. First, the very irrelevance of the sphere of ideas to practical aspects of social life, especially when coupled with the characteristic indifference of intellectuals toward the social implications of their contemplative questionings, invites accusations of "irresponsibility" not only from the general public but also from those intellectuals who are primarily concerned with material (ideological) interests, their own, those of other classes and strata, and occasionally the interests of the society as a whole. Second, pure thought is not merely indifferent to material interests; it can positively subvert the main vehicle of these interests within the realm of ideas, i.e., "ideologies." Pure intellectuality is averse to ideologies in general and to ideologies of intellectuals in particular. Of course, intellectuals are as likely as any other class to attempt legitimizing their material interests by creating their own ideologies. However, ideologies, as a set of relatively simple and fixed ideas in the service of a constellation of fixed material interests, are vulnerable to intellectualization; they will not last long if their central assumptions are constantly questioned, developed, pushed to their logical conclusions, or in short "rationalized." Rationalization, however, happens to be the essence of intellectuality; it is so central to intellectuals' ideal interests that they are expected to resist its adulteration for the sake of their material interests or in the name of ideological contingencies of anyone including their own. In arresting the evolution of ideas, all ideologies are bound eventually to appear to intellectuals as unwieldy impediments blocking the flow of ideas and their continuing rationalization.

The results of this tension appear on two levels:

1. On the personal level, this tension generates profound ambivalence. Intellectuals often face the dilemma of having to choose between intellectual integrity and extraintellectual contingencies, between rationalizing flow of ideas and dogmatic stagnation. Any decision in favor of the latter involves a "sacrifice of intellect." The concept of sacrifice of intellect is developed by Weber in the context of his sociology of religion (Weber, *Rejections*, p. 352; *India*, pp. 297–309). It characterizes an attempt by intellectuals to self-manage their unbridled quest for the socially destructive and ideologically deconstructive "truths." In the present context, it seems reasonable to assume that a sacrifice of intellect is called for not only when accommodating to extraneous circumstances—such as the demands of mass religiosity in India and those of orthodox Christianity in Europe—but also when intellectuals choose their own material interests over their ideal ones.

2. On the social level, the dilemma appears as a universal schism between ideologies and counterideologies of intellectuals. Intellectuals are at once the ablest of all groups to construct self-serving ideologies and the least likely to preserve them against internal strife. A Weberian sociology of intellectuals postulates an unrelenting strain between intellectuals' ideal and material interests, which is translated into the tension between intellectuals' "ideas" and "ideologies." Those "idealist" observers who ignore the material interests and ideological aspects of intellectuality, transcending them above the sphere of particular interests (e.g., Plato, Ward, Comte, and Mannheim), are as apt to miss the critical conflict of ideal and material interests as those of the "class analytic" school who by drawing on the thesis of social determination of consciousness ascribe ideological character to all of intellectuals' ideas (e.g., Bakunin, Machajski, Luxemburg, and Gouldner). Above all, neither of the two perspectives can account for the universal schism within the ranks of intellectuals, the perpetual debate between their ideologies and counterideologies. If the foregoing is valid, it would seem to follow that a radical asymmetry separates ideologies of all classes and strata, including those of an intelligentsia, from the ideologies of intellectuals: *ideologies of intellectuals are inherently unstable.*

By contrast, the intelligentsia's relationship to their ideologies is less fraught with tensions. As members of a less reflective stratum, one that is more geared to practical, rather than theoretical reason, the intelligentsia are more apt to build, preserve, and popularize ideologies. The intelligentsia has therefore exerted an enormous influence on the course of history through "reinterpreting" ideas generated by intellectuals, by accommodating them to common (social) or particular (class) interests. By virtue of being educated, the intelligentsia can think rigorously about ideas; because they are more distant from the flux of ideas, they can maintain their focus on the practical ramifications of ideas. The affinity of intelligentsia for ideologies, however, is not merely opportunistic. Because they are less reflective, members of the intelligentsia are more prone to internalize ideological constructions and less able to question or transcend their socially and culturally determined consciousness. As a result, the intelligentsia are more "at home" in any particular culture than are the intellectuals, whose very universal aspirations and socially irrelevant, deconstructive, or outright destructive musings render them untrustworthy: intellectuals are inherently a universally alien and alienated caste.

Having briefly delineated the conceptual differences between intellectuals and intelligentsia and their differential relationships to the sphere of ideas and ideologies, let us examine the historical significance of this theory for Weber's prognosis of Western civilization's objective possibilities. Studying past civilizations and observing the trends of his times, Weber grew pessimistic about the future of occidental individuality, which he cherished as one of the most valued achievements of Western civilization. He thought that the fate of individuality would be decided, among other things, by a decisive confrontation between intellectuals and intelligentsia. Weber had already observed that the consolidation of the intelligentsia in the vast state bureaucracies of Mesopotamia and the Orient had led to mass enslavement of their inhabitants. The autonomy of the individual in modern Western societies, as a unique product of the dawn of capitalism, was in the same vein threatened by the development of corporate capital as well as by the emergence of socialism. The latter represented the logical conclusion, rather than the antithesis of the former. Weber was persuaded that both capitalism and socialism carry the germs of a modern "Orientosis," that is, they are to varying degrees detrimental to individuality. This sociological insight informed Weber's harsh criticism of the bureaucratization of politics and fueled his resentment of the ideologies of the intelligentsia. To counterbalance the hegemony of the intelligentsia, Weber turned to the intellectuals. Neither his epistemological views regarding separation of facts and values that undermine those intellectual ideologies that link scholastic knowledge and public good, nor his critique of the irresponsibility and naiveté of intellectuals dabbling in politics, inhibited Weber's endorsement of intellectuals as champions of individuality. He encouraged them to enter politics not as a group of complacent "savants" or politically naive visionaries but as individuals keenly aware of the unique challenge of their political calling. This endorsement, occurred *in spite of* all the aforementioned misgivings not *because of* Weber's interest in seeing intellectuals empowered. It is appropriate to provide at this juncture a historical ideal type for the ideologies as well as counterideologies of the occidental intellectuals in order to underline Weber's unique reformulation of the mission of intellectuals in the political horizon of the modern world.

Bases for Ideologies of Occidental Intellectuals: An Ideal Type

Alvin Gouldner attributed a "Platonic complex" (ubiquitous unrequited yearning to become philosopher-kings) to occidental intellectuals (Gouldner, 1979, pp. 65–81). This claim is incorrect not only because it glosses over the tradition of Western anti-intellectualism but also because it overlooks the theoretical differences between classical and modern ideologies of intellectuals. Nonetheless it might be worthwhile to provide an alternative answer to the problem that lies at the root of Gouldner's question: "What, if anything, is the common denominator of the Western ideologies of intellectuals?"

The common presuppositions of Western ideologies of intellectuals from Plato to Lukacs can be reduced to the following three propositions.

1. There must exist a basic agreement on what we may call an ontological and epistemological *monism*. The belief that behind contradictory opinions and false (or chaotic) appearances lies the universally valid "truth" (or pattern) and that this truth is accessible to human reason.

2. It must be deemed that the truth is socially relevant. Knowledge of truth then becomes positively ameliorating if not categorically indispensable for the social and political life of human beings.

3. A belief must prevail that the intellectuals as carriers of this truth, having become its "vessels," must and will naturally aspire to act as its selfless "instruments."

Ideologies of intellectuals, however, have never gone unchallenged. The two-pronged challenge is typically launched by the intellectuals themselves. Among the ranks of intellectuals one can always find agnostics and skeptics who utterly reject all of the aforementioned premises. In this sense agnosticism is the most unfertile ground for ideologies in general. The sophistic rejection of "justice" as a universal and self-legitimizing principle must be first rejected if a "republic" of intellectuals is to be envisioned. Yet what we have termed "counterideologies of intellectuals," i.e., those sets of organized arguments designed to counter the claims of intellectuals to sovereignty, are rarely agnostic. This sort óf cynicism does not usually generate a zeal to counter the ideologies of intellectuals; the agent of this kind of "nihilism" might withdraw from the political arena altogether or remain in it with the intention of exploiting it all the more viciously in the absence of normative compunctions, for realizing personal or ideological goals. This is true of both ancient and postmodern discourses of intellectuals. Rather than denying the existence of truth or its accessibility (the first premise), counterideologies of intellectuals cast doubt on the problem of practical relevance of this knowledge (the second premise), and they especially relish exposing the tacit assumptions of selflessness of intellectuals as agents of collective good (the third premise).

By "ideologies of intellectuals" we mean those claims that aim to secure absolute sovereignty for intellectuals excluding from this category what might be called "weaker claims" that call for limited empowerment of those intellectuals who "naturally" rise to positions of power in a meritocratic environment. Although the weaker claims share something of the basic optimism of the ideologies of intellectuals about the selflessness of intellectual elites, such social thinkers as, for example, John Stuart Mill (1986, pp. 123–125, 182–187), James Madison (1961), and Karl Mannheim (1936, pp. 153–164), must be differentiated from the advocates of absolute sovereignty of intellectuals. Only the latter fits our ideal type of "ideologies of intellectuals." Indeed, among those who merely praise the intellectual elite as the forerunners and the stars of the political arena and encourage their participation in an open process of political representation, one finds such social thinkers as William Graham Sumner, Karl Popper, and, of course, Max Weber, all of whom passionately campaigned against the despotism of the enlightened elites.

The classical claim to sovereignty of intellectuals found its first and most eloquent expression in the platonic dialogues, especially in "The Republic," "Gorgias," and "Statesman." The style of Socratic and platonic discourse allows a glimpse of the radical skepticism of such sophists and orators as Thrasymachus, Gorgias, and Callicles, who denied that beyond opinion lies the universal, philosophically accessible, and socially relevant truth; and that the allegedly just and enlightened philosophers who claim to possess truth would be best suited to rule.

In each step, while explaining the basic identity of truth, knowledge, and the "good" to establish the wisdom of the rule of the wise against the claims of the strong (tyranny) and the many (democracy), Plato's Socrates encountered his interlocutors by putting forth a series of analogies. He argued, for instance, that the idea of good generates, makes possible, and shares a common identity with truth and knowledge in the same way that the sun generates, makes possible, and shares a basic identity with light and sight (Plato, 1968, Book 6, Par. 509a). Also the philosophically attainable knowledge of justice is equated to the science of medicine, and society to a living organism in crisis, thus elevating the philosopher-king to the status of a physician who administers bitter but beneficial potions. This position relegates orators (professional politicians) who vie for public approval to the status of cooks and confectioners who pander to the base desires of the feeble-minded masses who prefer delectable morsels to healthy and medicinal nourishment (Plato, 1968, Book 3, Par. 389b.c; 1971, Par. 460–463, 504, 521–522). To allow the ignorant masses to rule themselves through these politicians would lead to a republic of licentiousness and laxity that dispenses "a certain equality to equals and non-equals alike" and ultimately to "Democracy," i.e., the dictatorship of the poor and the uneducated (Plato, 1968, Book 8, Par. 557–558). This antidemocratic view of the first Western ideology of intellectuals is best summarized by Leo Strauss:

> Wisdom appeared to the classics as that title which is highest according to nature. It would be absurd to hamper the free flow of wisdom by any regulations; hence the rule of the wise must be absolute rule. It would be equally absurd to hamper the free flow of wisdom by consideration of the unwise wishes of the unwise; hence the wise rulers ought not to be responsible to their unwise subjects. To make the rule of the wise dependent on election by the unwise or consent of the unwise would mean to subject what is by nature higher to control by what is by nature lower, i.e., to act against nature. (Strauss, 1953, pp. 140–141)

Having established the attainability and social relevance of the "truth," Plato turned to the question of agency. His rejection of the possibility of abusing political power for personal gain rather than using it in the service of the social order is tautological. He assumed that "a man who has learnt about right will be righteous" (Plato, 1971, Par. 460), and that genuine arts such as those possessed by the philosopher-king, pilot, physician, and shepherd (unlike spurious arts such as cooking and oratory) are by definition "unabusable" (Plato, 1968, Book 1 Par. 340–345). In the famous platonic parable of the cave, the philosopher alone breaks away from the world of false shadows to catch a glimpse of "realities." It is this privileged access to the gnosis (*Sophia*), not a claim to expertise and practical knowledge (*phrenosis*), that enables him to lead the denizens of the cave away from their illusions and cure their spiritual as well as social ills.

In contrast, Aristotle classified the science of politics under practical wisdom (*phrenosis*) together with ethics and technology, rather than associating it with the pure philosophic reasoning that generates mathematics, natural science, and theology (Aristotle,

1979, Book 6, Par. 5). Yet the implementation of practical wisdom presupposed that the aim of politics is to lead the society of men in order to promote what inhered in human nature and to provide the "good life" for its citizens (Aristotle, 1982, Par. 1252b27–1253al). But as the knowledge of this presupposes considerable intellectual preparation, Aristotle could also be said to tacitly propose the rule of the virtuous intellectuals. The "genuine" state concerns itself with promoting "virtue" or else it is nothing but a military alliance in which "law" becomes a mere agreement (or a social contract) (Aristotle, 1982, Par. 1280a34–1281a7).

The classics viewed history as either the record of social entropy and increasing chaos or a haphazard jumble of happenings that lacked rhyme or reason. Consequently the axis of the ideological debates between ideological and political intellectuals and their opponents revolved around a decisionist and historical choice between ideal and actual regimes.

As the moderns introduced reason and telos to history, the debate around the idea of social evolution became central to the ideologies and counterideologies of intellectuals. The assumption of social evolution in the modern debate (that continued within the traditions of sociology and socialism) performed the same function that the ideas of truth and goodness once had in classical times. Also entirely irrational views of history in which the absolute leaders were entrusted with the task of arbitrarily shaping the fate of nations also continued to exist and even flourish, attracting groups of antirational intellectuals. Rejection of substantive reason reproduced a replica of the ancient sophistic praise of power.[2]

Notwithstanding its historical importance, this trend failed to capture the imagination of more than a few isolated intellectuals or to significantly alter the modern rational view of history commonly shared by ideologies and counterideologies of intellectuals. Since the existence of social evolution was taken for granted by all, the crucial fault line dividing the ideologies and counterideologies of intellectuals occurred primarily along the idea of "automaticity" of social evolution. A fully automated social evolution would undermine the legitimacy of claims to leadership by the knowledge elite in the name of corrective intervention. A semiautomatic process, however, would introduce enough irrationality into the otherwise rational progression of history to legitimize political ambitions of the professing "midwives of social change," "social engineers," "ameliorating experts," "savants," and "sociocrats."

In the modern occidental West, ideologists of intellectuals have broadcast their views using a variety of sounding boards including French communal thought and, later, through French sociology. Counterideologists of intellectuals, on the other hand, have mainly used the intellectual arsenal of British political liberalism and, to a lesser degree, that of social Darwinism. The debate between the two sides continued in early American sociology. In the occidental East, the ideologies of intellectuals were reflected in Marxism and later in Bolshevism and Leninism while counterideologies of intellectuals borrowed from anarchism, as well as academic Marxism. Highlights of this debate are outlined in Appendix D.

In short, the locus of legitimizing claims of modern ideologies of intellectuals has shifted to new areas. Instead of claiming to have access to "absolute truths" and the putative relevance of such truths to "public good," the ideologists of intellectuals have vaunted radical social engineering in the cause of hastening the pace or correcting the direction of social evolution. On certain occasions they have even claimed to be the very agents of social evolution in its final stage. The modern claims may appear less ambitious than those made by classical ideologies of intellectuals except in one respect: whereas the classics maintained that the relationship between philosophy and sovereignty was a contingent and coincidental one, the modern "sociocrats" (Lester Frank Ward), "savants" (Auguste Comte), and "vanguards" (Lenin) deem the connection of knowledge and power as necessary (Bloom, 1968, p. 460). Modern anti-intellectual thought has decried the perceived subjugation of the citizens under the despotic rule of the intellectual elites. John Stuart Mill's critique of the Comtean system of positive politics and Bakunin's critical view of Marxist elitism reflect this resentment (John Stuart Mill, 1986, p. 73, Bakunin, 1972, p. 318).

Let us recall that the practical ramifications of this immanent tension between the ideal and material interests of intellectuals can be called upon to explain two historical phenomena: (1) a subjective ambivalence toward commitment to ideas or ideologies, and (2) an objective controversy between ideologies and counterideologies of intellectuals. In the absence of a hegemonic ideology of an intellectual elite, the modern occidental West (Western Europe and the

United States) has given rise to the subjective ambivalence of intellectuals. Western intellectuals have expressed this state of mind in a prolonged soliloquy on the relationship between power and intellect, with alternating undertones of optimistic enthusiasm, nostalgic distance, or ironic cynicism. Intellectuals in the occidental East, however, have been objectively split between the camps of ruling elites and the oppressed counterelites. The developments of a Marxist tradition in the geocultural sphere of Eastern Europe can provide us with generalizing insights into the objectification of the split between ideal and material interests of intellectuals. The material interest of the hegemonic circles of intellectual leaders reflected in the ideologies of sovereign intellectuals are easily expropriated by intelligentsia, transforming what started out as a civil war within the ranks of intellectuals into a class conflict between intelligentsia fortified in the machinery of the modern state and the increasingly disenfranchised intellectuals (possibly in alliance with other classes, namely, the proletariat). Raymond Aron observed: "Under a communist regime the intellectuals, sophists rather than philosophers, rule the roost" (Aron, 1962, p. 290).

Another interesting aspect of the objective split of intellectuality in Eastern Europe is the fact that the counterideologies of intellectuals continued to adhere to the core ideas of the ruling elites (ideas such as social determination of consciousness and social evolution through class conflict) rather than rejecting them. Having recovered these ideas from their ideological contexts, the intellectual counterelite attempted to restore the dogmatized concepts by revitalizing their intrinsic rationalizing tendencies, hoping that the mere life and movement of core ideas would implode hardened ideological shells built around them. As a heterodoxy they found a reliable ally in core ideas of their tradition; they discovered that advocating a new orthodoxy might be safer as well as a more efficient way of fighting the "dogma" and its defenders.

We have no reason to believe that the subjective ambivalence of intellectuals in respect to their ideal and material interests and the objectified version of it (i.e., the acrimony between ideologies and counterideologies of intellectuals) will subside or disappear. On the contrary, we believe that the rift is bound to exist because intellectuals' mastery of the world (the ultimate end of ideologies of intellectuals) is achieved at the expense of intellectual mastery of the world (the unhampered substantive and theoretical rationalization of the images of the world).

Weber and Ideologies of Intellectuals

Max Weber's philosophical predilections were unconducive to the ideal typical occidental ideology of intellectuals. First and foremost, Weber rejected ontological and epistemological monism that had long been accepted as staple presuppositions of most Western intellectual traditions. Second, by separating the spheres of intellectuality, morality, and politics, Weber severed the ideologically significant link between rationally discovered (or revealed) truth (or moral right) and political power. Nevertheless, Weber did not inveigh against intellectuals' aspirations for public life. After all, he left open (especially for intellectuals) the possibility of transcending individual and sectarian interests. Weber was keenly aware of the problems that could arise when intellectuals decide to dabble in politics. Yet his very attempt to rectify intellectuals' attitudes toward politics, for instance, in "Politics as a Vocation," presupposes an assumption of basic corrigibility of intellectuals' naive encounter with politics. In his political writings, Weber sneered at those intellectuals who would try to monopolize state power as a class, but he also hailed them as potentially powerful individual politicians. It is to such leaders that Weber entrusted the task of defending the dignity of the individual in what he perceived to be the coming crisis of Western civilization.

This endorsement, however, can hardly land Weber in the camp of the ideologists of the intellectuals. He could not belong there because of his "ontological" opposition to the monism of the occidental intellectuality. Weber's metatheoretical assumptions are inspired by James Mill's axiom: "If one proceeds from pure experience one arrives at polytheism" (Weber, *Science*, p. 147; *Meanings*, p. 17). Weber had observed that in the sphere of religion, the rationalizing propensities of intellectuals promoted transcendental monotheism. Where this was not possible, intellectuals led efforts to organize the autonomous functional or local demigods in a hierarchically ordered pantheon. Against the backdrop of his

polytheistic social ontology, Weber judged these efforts to be ultimately self-defeating (see Chapter 2) (Weber, *Economy I*, pp. 407,
410, 419, 518; *India*, p. 152; *Judaism*, pp. 153, 154).

Max Weber's social polytheism was absolute; it could not be
compromised, at least not in the true sense of the word (Weber,
Meaning, pp. 17, 18). Futile attempts to wish away the utterly
irreconcilable "spheres of value" could only aggravate the inner
struggle of these spheres (Weber, *Rejections*, p. 328). Universalist
religions undertook to dissolve the local and tribal religious boundaries and ultimately collapsed the spheres of politics, morality,
religion, etc. We have already alluded to the Weberian paradox of
"over-rationalization" in the religious sphere: the most rationally
consistent theodicies are the most useless, as in their flawless consistency they cease to correspond to a world that is commonly experienced as suffused with contradictions and inequities. The duality
between the order pervading the rational sphere of abstract thought
and the chaos of "reality" that resists logical order may also be
found in the world of politics. Attempts to rationalize the social
world and to bring under control the human conduct are also
doomed: "In politics, as in economics, the more rational the political order became the sharper the problems of these tensions became" (Weber, *Politics*, p. 333). It was Weber's conviction that
intellectuals who enter politics had better honestly admit that most
of the radical problems that arise in political life are ultimately
unresolvable by human reason, or that there is more than one
rational solution.

Weber's assumption of separate value spheres would also challenge the second premise of the ideologies of intellectuals (commensurability of "truth" into social policy). More than the contradictions within value spheres, the abysmal void that separates them
would undermine intellectuals' claim to "know" the common good
or to represent it. In a Weberian universe, where unity and meaning
are only subjective and where spheres of life contradict one another
in every possible way, questions of social policy can be settled only
by the democratic selection of prerational choices, not by recourse
to a universally applicable"science." In his critique of Roscher,
Weber criticized a version of platonic medical allegory that likened
social policy to a form of "therapy" aimed at curing the "ailing
society." Weber argued that to treat economic policy as therapy

would require the definition of normal social state of health and the demonstration of the conduciveness of the ostensibly self-evident social policies to the cause of social well-being (Weber, *Roscher*, p. 87, 88). According to Weber, economic theories are merely useful ideal typical constructions based on presuppositions whose deceptive "self-evidence" must be taken with a grain of salt (see Chapter 1). The "meaning adequacy" of an ideal type (as we have already argued in the first chapter) must not replace empirical research to ascertain its "causal adequacy." Only at the expense of profound self-deception could one assume that economic theories portray an adequate picture of innately good and bad policies or that they can spare one the difficulty of making a choice (Weber, *Meaning*, pp. 19, 36, 44). Weber attempted to demonstrate the ideological nature of "scientific social planning" by tracing its academic popularity to the increasing encroachment of the state in the economic sphere and its concomitant influence on the character of universities, which had started to become mere training grounds for state officials (Weber, *Meaning*, p. 45). It is obvious that for Weber empirical sciences could not dictate what one "should" do, nor could universities pretend to impart such knowledge: "An empirical science cannot tell anyone what he *should* do—but rather what he *can* do—and under certain circumstances—what he wishes to do" (Weber, *Objectivity*, p. 54). The universities can only "sharpen the student's capacity to . . . think clearly and 'to know what one wants.' . . . Everything else—the entire substance of his aspirations and goals—the individual must achieve for himself." (Weber, *Freedom*, p. 21).

Now that we have underlined Weber's rejection of the monistic assumption common to most ideologies of intellectuals as well as his profound doubts regarding the commensurability of a scientific "truth" to a scientific social policy (the first and second assumptions of ideologies of intellectuals), let us concentrate on the question of agency. Although Weber's separation of facts and values and his assumption of separate and potentially antagonistic spheres of intellectuality, morality, and politics militate against ideologies of intellectuals, he did not share the pessimism of ancient sophists or that of modern anarchists about the intellectuals' willingness or ability to transcend their self-interest and prejudices. Even when considering such phenomena as the facility with which formerly radical intellectuals turn into authoritarian officials of the rightist and leftist movements, Weber appealed to their social psychology rather than tracing this metamorphosis to the intellectuals' sinister will to power or their desire to realize their material interests. This apparently radical transmutation of the intellectuals' social character did not signify for Weber any "innate disposition or ignoble self-seeking on their part." Rather it indicated their "pragmatic rationalism," their "yearning for 'action' in the service of absolute social and ethical values." Such romantic yearning could then be translated into reactionary or revolutionary authoritarianism depending on whether it started from above or from below (Weber, *Russia*, p. 271). Weber's motivational analysis of revolutionary or reactionary intellectuals also found expression in his essay on socialism. He did not view socialism as an ominous plot that motivates intellectuals to seize control of the political machine in order to realize class interests. Rather, intellectuals join the socialist movement because of "the *romance* of the general strike and the romance of the hope of revolution as such which fascinates them. One can tell by looking at them that they are romantics" (Weber, *Socialism*, p. 215). These instances indicate that Weber was more concerned with intellectuals' naiveté and emotional immaturity than their hidden agenda to usurp power and rule as self-seeking despots.

Of course, Max Weber shared with the sophistic and agnostic anti-intellectual tradition a basic rejection of the possibility of intellectuals' achieving and applying the politically relevant truths. This, as we have already mentioned, is contrary to the credo of counterideologies of intellectuals as well (they accept most of the philosophical premises of intellectual ideologies preferring to cast doubt on the question of "agency"). Weber is far from being a champion of the agnostics' anti-intellectualism, nor is he an advocate of the traditional Western counterideologies of intellectuals. It is true that he rejected the philosophical premises of intellectuals' collective ideologies and repudiated their ideological claims. Yet, notwithstanding his reservations, Weber encouraged participation of intellectuals in politics as individuals and individualists; he even appeared eager to entrust the future of individuality to them. Who could better represent the cause of individuality than the most reflective members of the society? Intellectuals come closest to the conscious life of an individual to the extent that they distance themselves from the realms of "habitual" and "traditional" action. But Weber also had a major qualm about this: if intellectuals are to carry the torch of individuality in the impending "polar night" of Western civilization, they need to mend their ways. The endemic problem for politically active intellectuals was their political dilettantism and their "irresponsibility." Thus Weber attempted to warn them against the dangers that awaited them in the arena of politics. We will come back to this topic later in this chapter to underline the substance of Weber's advice to intellectuals.

Bases for Ideologies of Intelligentsia: An Ideal Type

The claim that practical wisdom imparted through formal education is indispensable for the smooth functioning of the government is a necessary component of the ideologies of intelligentsia. In order to secure claims to political power, however, the intelligentsia is bound to develop or adopt substantive arguments concerning the nature of the state and its apparatus. As vehicles of modern ideologies of intelligentsia, socialism and the welfare state claim to serve the individual and promote the commonweal through performing rational redistributive functions. Max Weber had serious misgivings about both of these forms of government.

Weber's negative attitude toward the claims of the welfare state were informed by his comparative historical study of the Indian, Chinese, and near Eastern empires in whose vast state bureaucracies the intelligentsia rose to ascendancy. The root of the modern welfare state, in Weber's view, bifurcates into two separate ideas of *material* and *spiritual* welfare. The former was a constant component of patrimonial bureaucracies of China, India, and Mesopotamia. The two basic ideas of "kingly charity" and "appeal to heaven" were closely related to the ideal of a welfare state as a protectorate of the dispossessed masses. The possibility of direct "appeal to heaven" by the downtrodden and the destitute, i.e., the ruler's fear of the "curse of the poor," was supposed to check the absolutism of the king and ensure a modicum of justice for the masses. But it also served the kingly interest by protecting his taxpayers against the brutality of his officials (Weber, *Judaism*, pp. 256–257).[3]

In India and China, we also encounter the general idea of a welfare state as the guarantor of the material welfare of the subjects. However, it was in India that for the first time the king undertook to provide not only material but also spiritual welfare for his subjects. It was not the goal of King Ashuka's welfare policies merely to "augment the number of tax payers and the capacity to pay taxes" but to care for people in order that they be "happy" and "attain heaven" as well (Weber, *India*, p. 242). In China, the cleavage between welfare ideologies based on purely material grounds and those promoting both material and spiritual welfare of the subjects remained unbridged (Weber, *China*, p. 137). This cleavage was partly due to the opposition of two Chinese intellectual traditions. On one side, a powerful alliance was formed between ruling intellectuals who advised the pontiff and the bureaucratic intelligentsia who ran the empire. Having had at their disposal an official philosophy (Confucianism) as well as culturally stereotyped molds for the carriers of this philosophy (the literati), Chinese imperial bureaucracy sought to expand the realm of legitimate intervention of the state. The Taoist tradition, however, remained skeptical of the literati's efforts to manage the material and spiritual lives of the masses. The Taoists charged that the Confucian literati had not taken the "naturally" unequal intellectual and spiritual endowments of the subjects seriously. The literati had maintained that through "education" the rabble could be elevated to the highest possible levels of sophistication. Against this belief the Taoists held that the state must not interfere with what is unchangeable in the cosmic and social order and that the leveling of the unequal charismatic endowments that legitimized the "aristocracy of grace" was wrong. "The rulers may fill their subjects' bellies not their minds; they may strengthen their limbs but not their character" (Weber, *China*, pp. 187–88).

The more recent avatars of the warring gods of state interventionism, the radical moral equalitarianism (from Rousseau to Bakunin), on the one side, and the meritocratic system of respecting and cultivating natural differences (British liberal philosophers and economists), on the other, are as little inclined to cease fighting in modern times as they were in ancient China (Weber, *China*, p. 137; *Meaning*, p. 15).

One of the functions of a welfare state is to formalize and legitimize the status opposition between cultured elites and uncultured masses by developing an organic image for social order. "Such ideas," Weber stated, "suggest themselves to any political welfare organization" (Weber, *India*, p. 143). Hence the similarity of ideologies of all welfare states. Although the objective possibility of the development of an organismic social order did not materialize in the Chinese welfare state (due to the strength of Chinese guilds and sibs), Weber perceived elective affinities between the two and cautioned against the development of such ideologies in the future. An organismic social order would set the stage for mass enslavement by fettering the individual to his job, class and occupation (Weber, *Economy II*, p. 1402). At this juncture the bureaucrat is in a paradoxical position: he is harnessed into the human machine as a "cog" and "chained" to his activity, yet he has a vested interest in seeing the mechanism and its authority perpetuated (Weber, *Bureaucracy*, p. 228). As such, the bureaucrat is the first inmate in the house of bondage that he is building.

Weber was not enthusiastic about the modern welfare state and its proponents. Their apparent concern for the well-being of individuals appeared to him as anachronistic if not merely ideological (Weber, *Rejections*, p. 334). Such "concerns" appeared to him either as reflecting the special interests of entrenched redistributive bureaucracies, or as concealing justifications for expansionism of the state per se (Weber, *Bureaucracy*, p. 213). Weber repeatedly warned against the apparently impartial and objective bureaucratic elites as harbingers of an "indestructible" dictatorship of the officials of the "Oriental-Egyptian type" (Weber, *Economy II*, p. 1402).

If Weber's critique of the capitalist welfare state was based on the study of the past, his rejection of socialism was based on an analysis of the present: "The 'socialism of the future' is a phrase for the rationalization of economic life by combining further bureaucratization and interest-group administration" (Weber, *Meaning*, p. 47). In other words, socialism represented a further rationalization of the capitalist system in which the worst aspects of the present system of capitalism, i.e., bureaucratization, would be augmented. Even if it were possible to bring about the total collapse of capitalism overnight, no doubt a sweet dream of many socialists, the question would remain: "Who would then take control of and direct this new economy?" (Weber, *Socialism*, p. 262). The dictatorship of the official, not that of the worker, would be the result of socialism. This would entrench the intelligentsia in power, dashing forever the hopes of rekindling the lights of freedom and individuality in the Occident. The configurations of the alliances at the moment of the collapse of Eastern European socialism vindicate not only Weber's prognoses of the inherent weaknesses of socialism but also of the respective relationships of intellectuals and intelligentsia to the centralized state.

Weber and Ideologies of Intelligentsia

Weber's case against ideologies of intelligentsia is based on three arguments: the impossibility of using expert knowledge to resolve socioeconomic problems, the narrow and often unmediated class interests of the carriers of this "knowledge," and the impending peril of bureaucratic domination under postliberal capitalist[4] or socialist regimes.

Weber's critique of the technocratic elites professing to have reduced questions of socioeconomic policy to a "science" overlaps his basic antipathy to the ideologies of intellectuals. We have already observed that Weber's neo-Kantian epistemology and his polytheistic social ontology exclude logical ratiocination as a means of solving socioeconomic and ultimately political problems. On this basis, Weber argued that what purported to be the newly discovered "laws" of economics could arrive at unambiguous "social policies" only at the expense of treating a number of their presuppositions as self-evident (Weber, *Meaning*, pp. 36–38). We have also pointed out that Weber was aware of, and warned against the spurious "self-evidence" of ideal types. The laws of economics, being nothing but another set of ideal types, might also give the appearance of self-evidence. This is why Weber preferred that the questions of social policy be "disputed" publicly rather than "solved" as technical problems.

The adulation of a sacralized, scientific approach to social problems would also tend to hide the ideological bias of the so-called scientific economists. According to Weber, even if a scientific approach could arrive at undisputable social policies, the narrow, unmediated class interest of the intelligentsia who would claim to represent it would almost certainly contour it to serve their own narrow interests. Here Weber appears to fully endorse the Marxist axiom of social determination of consciousness as well as the ideological nature of social sciences. Max Weber's radical theory of social conflict at once emphasizes and goes beyond the Marxian scheme of class conflict:

> The conflict occurs not merely . . . between "class interests" but between general views on life and the universe as well. This latter point, however, does not lessen the truth that the particular ultimate value judgments which the individual espouses is decided among other factors and certainly to a quite significant degree by the degree of affinity between it and class interests. (Weber, *Objectivity*, p. 56)

It goes without saying, however, that Weber applies the Marxist class analysis more readily to the intelligentsia than to intellectuals. It would be not only philosophically naive but also sociologically ingenuous to assume that a stratum of technocrats can and will resolve and implement all social, economic, and political questions impartially and scientifically. Of course, it must be emphasized that unlike Marx, Weber subscribed to the liberal ideal of a transcendental politics, i.e., a political realm least manipulated for particularistic economic interests of the politicians. Instead of postulating this kind of politics as the natural state of affairs in all liberal democracies, however, Weber treated it as problematic and asked about the conditions of its actualization. He asked: What kind of agency would best achieve the autonomy of the political realm? For instance, classes or strata that were on the decline (Junkers) or on the rise (entrepreneurs) were least able or willing to transcend their economic interests in favor of genuine political solutions. Certain professionals among intellectuals (e.g., lawyers), however, were better fitted sociologically and economically to enter politics, as they could afford to live "for" politics not "off" of it (Weber, *Politics*, pp. 84–85).

Intellectuals "can" formulate political agendas and defend them with (measured) conviction. By contrast, the intelligentsia would be least likely to engage in "true" (transcendental) politics. Weber deemed the careerism of the bureaucrats to be antithetical to the qualities of commitment to ideals and political responsibility that were, from his point of view, indispensable for the political calling.

In applying what amounted to a sober Marxist class analysis to bureaucracy, Weber disenchanted the future utopias of both liberal and socialist "literati." To dispel the liberal "Pollyannaish" praise of bureaucratization, Weber pointed out that the growth of capitalism and bureaucracy neither promotes nor parallels democratization. On the contrary: such growth among other "weather signs" points in the direction of "increasing unfreedom." Weber held it to be "utterly ridiculous" to equate the development of modern capitalism with "freedom," "democracy," or individualism. Indeed, he asked himself, "How are all these things [i.e., freedom, democracy and individualism] in general and in the long term *possible* where it (i.e., modern capitalism) prevails?" (Weber, *Russia*, p. 282). To the extent that modern bureaucracy, as a "power instrument of the first order" is increasingly rationalized and rendered more indispensable and more "unshatterable," it becomes antithetical to liberal ideals (Weber, *Bureaucracy*, pp. 228–231; *Economy II*, p. 1401). The dynamics of developing capitalism and bureaucracy do not promote freedom. If anything, it is the voluntaristic "*will* of a nation not to allow itself to be led like a flock of sheep" that may guarantee freedom and individuality (Weber, *Russia*, p. 282).

Weber brought the gift of Marxist class analysis not only to the bourgeois flatterers of bureaucracy but also to the Marxist ideologists of the proletarian state. In his essay on socialism, Weber focused on the blind spot of Marxist movements of his time; he proffered a class analysis of the bureaucratization of the Marxist movement and of its consequences. He maintained that those who lived "off" Social Democracy, from innkeepers whose establishments are patronized by radicals, to university professors, editors, party officials, etc., would not abandon their vested interests for the sake of revolutionary believers and their beliefs (Beetham, 1985, p. 162). "Nothing is further from the thoughts of this class than solidarity with the proletariat, they are much more concerned with increasing the gap between the proletariat and themselves" (Weber, *Socialism*, p. 261).

The ultimate naiveté of both the liberal and radical panegyrists of bureaucratization consisted in that they were applauding the inevitable process of bureaucratization, not realizing that their applause was itself a part of that process: "The future belongs to bureaucratization, and it is evident that in this regard the literati pursue their calling—to provide a salvo of applause to the up-and-coming powers—just as they did in the age of laissez-faire, both times with the same naiveté" (Weber, *Economy II*, p. 1401). Max Weber's political views were as profoundly influenced by his vision of the future as they were informed by his study of the past.

To describe Weber's critique of the future of the Occident we have coined the word "Orientosis." It would be consistent with Weber's views on cross-cultural understanding to assert that he confronted non-Western civilizations with questions that were primarily relevant to the Western societies. But the reverse was also true: Weber used the insights he had gained through his comparative historical studies as an integral part of his political sociology. By fusing the objective possibilities of the present with certain historical ideal types, Weber arrived at a prognosis of the trends of his time, which became central to his political ideals. Weber identified with the Jewish prophets of doom partly because he felt that he had seen the future of the Occident in the past of the Orient and Mesopotamia. This helped Weber replace the vague pessimistic futurology of Toqueville and Mill with his vivid prophecy of doom: "Everywhere, the *casing of the new serfdom* is ready" (Weber, *Socialism*, p. 281). Socialism, far from being an alternative destination, was a shortcut to the "iron cage." The subjugation of the individual would become complete sooner if the machinery of private capitalism were to be dismantled and replaced by the central management of nationalized and socialized enterprises. Monopolization of the bureaucratic machine would create a latter-day version of mass enslavement in the style of ancient Egypt, except "it would occur in a much more rational—and hence unbreakable—form" (Weber, *Economy II*, p. 1402). Bureaucrats are particularly earmarked to keep the gates of the "house of bondage" of the future. The animated machine of bureaucracy," together with the inanimate machine . . . is busy fabricating the shell of bondage which men will perhaps be forced to inhabit someday, as powerless as the fellahs of ancient Egypt" (Weber, *Economy II*, p. 1402). The socialists were mistaken to think that their state bureaucracy was any better than its capitalist (private or public) counterparts. On the one hand, socialism would inevitably proliferate bureaucracies in order to take over nationalized corporations. On the other, it would eliminate the competition of private bureaucracies, and that between private and public bureaucracies, leaving the way open for total control of the civil society by a centralized state machine.

Weber credited American workers for seeing through the bureaucratic peril, rejecting "civil service reform." They "preferred to be governed by parvenus of doubtful morality rather than a formally qualified mandarinate" (Weber, *Russia*, p. 282). In the impending orientalization of the Occident, a new bureaucracy would be created more powerful and stifling than those of Egypt and China. The question was: What could be done to prevent this?

Weber's Political Agenda:
Democracy, Bureaucracy, and Mass Societies

Like Alexis de Tocqueville and John Stuart Mill, Weber revered the autonomy of the individual and dreaded the impending demise of individuality and freedom in the flowing tide of mass equalitarianism and total bureaucratization (Mill, 1986, pp. 59–63, 121-123; Tocqueville, 1969, pp. 250–262). Unlike them, however, Weber had a clear vision of the nature of this threat. Weber's theory of increasing orientalization of the Occident integrates his comparative sociology with a form of futurology based on an estimate of objective possibilities for occidental civilization. This bleak premonition went a long way to temper Weber's liberal convictions and affect his political agenda. His view of liberal democracy and its institutions was an instrumental one; the whole system could be used to protect individuality and the hegemony of the state through its bureaucratic machine. Despite apparent elective affinities between democratization and the growth of bureaucracy, Weber maintained that they are fundamentally incompatible:

> We must remember the fact which we have encountered several times and which we shall have to discuss repeatedly: that "democracy" as such is opposed to the "rule" of bureaucracy, in spite and perhaps because of its unavoidable yet unintended promotion of bureaucratization. Under certain conditions, democracy creates palpable breaks in the bureaucratic pattern and impediments to bureaucratic organization. (Weber, *Economy II*, p. 991)

People in a mass society are confronted with the colossal human machine of bureaucracy, which functions as an instrument of power for the state while furthering the interests of its members through the control of information (official secrecy) and practical knowledge. Even the masters of bureaucracy, be they "the people," oligarchies, or tyrants, find themselves as powerless as clumsy dilettantes trying to use a sophisticated machine to further their own causes. Under liberal democratic regimes, however, the control and containment of bureaucracy seem to be better institutionalized: reason enough to prefer such social systems to any form of centralized control.

Before elaborating on the superiority of democratic institutions in checking the power of bureaucracies, it must be stated that Weber's emphasis on the problems of bureaucratic control does not mean that he was solely concerned with the threat of a bureaucratic intelligentsia, but that he feared them as a more immediate threat to the ideals of freedom and individuality in the West. Centralism either under the intellectuals (e.g., Jacobism or Marxism) or under the intelligentsia (e.g., state bureaucracies of socialism and capitalism) were seen by Weber as equally inimical to the growth of the autonomous individual (Weber, *Russia*, p. 281).

As we suggested earlier, Weber's abhorrence of centralism by or in the name of the people links him to the romantic liberalism of John Stuart Mill (Mill, 1986, pp. 184–185). While his critical distance from such concepts as "the inalienable rights of man" sets him apart from classical liberalism, there is no doubt that Weber nonetheless jealously treasured these "inalienable human rights"—apparently as useful myths—and was adamant that the private sphere be protected from the incursions of the state (Weber, *Russia*, p. 283). It also is true that like classical liberals Weber deemed the goal of democratic control of the state to be the protection of the inchoate seeds of individuality in the West. Yet, probably the most important aspect of Weber's liberalism is that he did not stop at expounding his ideals—or portending his prophecies of doom—but proceeded to offer concrete political guidelines in order to reconcile them with the realities of mass society and its increasing bureaucratization. Weber also attempted to integrate his own theory of social conflict (between and within social classes as well as among value spheres) with his liberal ideals. The result is a particular blend of ideas and ideals that initiated a new era in liberal thought of the twentieth century.

As Socrates is credited with calling philosophy from heaven and bringing it to earth, so should Weber be recognized as the thinker who brought the ideals of individualism and freedom from the heaven of classical and romantic liberalism to the mundane world of mass democracies. Weber was not the only liberal for whom individuality and freedom came before equality and political participation, but he certainly is among the first to boldly formulate his ideas in the form of an elitist tradition within liberalism. Neglecting Weber, this trend is nowadays usually identified with a line of thinkers ranging from Schumpeter to Dahl (Macpherson, 1977, pp. 76–92).

Weber openly doubted the value of mass participation in the democratic process (Weber, *Economy II*, pp. 1459–1460) and endorsed the so-called principle of small numbers:

> The broad mass of deputies functions only as a following for the leader or the few leaders who form the government, and it blindly follows them *as long as* they are successful. *This is the way it should be.* Political action is always determined by the "principle of small numbers," that means, the superior political maneuverability of small leading groups. *In mass states, this caesarist element is ineradicable* [italics added]. (Weber, *Economy II*, p. 1414)

Weber also rejected as contemptible the rule of mediocre intelligentsia in state and party bureaucracies under the guise of a mass leaderless democracy. These two facts drove him to advocate the charismatic leadership of a democratically elected leader. This "caesarist" element in Weber's political thought has been the subject of much controversy, which is not at issue here. It is, however, beyond doubt that for Weber, even under the most democratic form of state, the passivity of masses was a given: "It is not the politically passive 'mass' that produces the leader from its midst, but the political leader recruits his following and wins the mass through 'demagogy'" (Weber, *Economy II*, p. 1457). Weber did not require the liberal democratic parliament to be the voice of the masses; rather, these bodies were supposed to fulfill two practical functions. First, the parliament supplies a modicum of necessary rational legitimation for the modern state:

Modern parliaments are primarily representative bodies of those ruled with bureaucratic means. After all, a certain minimum of consent on the part of the ruled, at least of the socially important strata, is a precondition of the durability of every, even the best organized, domination. Parliaments are today the means of manifesting this minimum consent. (Weber, *Economy II*, pp. 1407–1408)

The second function of the parliament is to provide a countervailing force in order to check the power of the entrenched bureaucracy of the state. Though the necessity of "watchful criticism" of bureaucracy was already proposed by others (e.g., by Mill), it was Weber who depicted the institutional framework within which this could be accomplished.

Weber's Political Agenda: The Varieties of Irresponsibility

Weber was as averse to the total sovereignty of a handful of intellectuals as he was opposed to the hegemony of the bureaucratic intelligentsia as a class. Yet he chose intellectuals as his champions of political leadership while warning them against confounding their politics with maxims of ethical and rational intellectualization. To enter politics for an intellectual might be tantamount to giving up the search for symmetry and consistency of the intellectual and moral spheres without accepting the view of the hardened practitioners of "power politics." The intellectual who fails to adjust to the political calling becomes a "cosmic ethical rationalist," which Weber deems to be the most dangerous political animal. He believed that this sort of political intellectual would be easily overwhelmed by the ethical immorality of the world. In trying to remain loyal to a set of absolute and abstract moral or ideological principles, such a person will resort to wishful thinking: "from good comes only good, but from evil only evil follows," that is, one needs only to take stock of one's own intentions and rest assured that the results of an action will follow suit. Thus the visionary intellectual would become the paragon of "irresponsibility" (Weber, *Politics*, pp. 121–122). Such a breed of politically motivated intellectuals evoke the wrong paradigm in early Christianity when subscribing to the maxim of "Do right and leave the rest to God." Instead, Weber would advise them to take heart: The early Christians knew full well the world is governed by demons and that he who lets himself in for politics, that is, for power and force as means, contracts with diabolical powers and that for his action it is *not* true that good can follow only from good and evil only from evil, but that often the opposite is true (Weber, *India*, p. 184; *Politics*, p. 123).

   In spite of the berating of politicized intellectuals' political naiveté, despite calling some of them "windbags" and "backwoods politicians," and despite criticizing their "soft-headed" and "Philistine" attitude in trying to "replace the 'political' with the 'ethical,'" Weber continued to assume the ultimate corrigibility of the politically aspiring intellectuals. Why was he less generous with politicized bureaucratic intelligentsia? Because their "irresponsibility" was not the result of naiveté or idealism; it was an integral part of their status ethos. "It is in the nature of officials of high moral standing to be poor politicians, and above all, in the political sense of the word, to be irresponsible politicians" (Weber, *Politics*, p. 95). At first sight the organized irresponsibility of the bureaucrats might seem benign when compared with the irresponsibility of the zealous intellectuals (e.g., syndicalists). The threat of the former, however, was seen by Weber to be an accomplished fact, in view of Germany's recent disastrous political events; it also appeared immanent, as following from the formal and practical rationalizing trends of Western civilization. Without underestimating the perils of intellectuals' participation in politics, Weber diagnosed the bureaucratic "organized irresponsibility" to be infinitely more pernicious and ultimately incurable. Therefore he did not set out to admonish the Prussian bureaucrats in the art of politics; "politics" was not a "vocation" he wished them to master. Instead, Weber attacked them by attributing to their "careerism" nearly all of the evils of German politics. The calling of a civil servant, Weber maintained, is to sacrifice his convictions to the demands of obedience. This is diametrically opposed to the calling of a politician. Weber's disapproving tone is unyielding:

> It is reliably known that almost all of the men who were in charge of our policies in that disastrous decade have time and again privately repudiated grave declarations for which they accepted formal responsibility. If one asked with amazement why a statesman remained

in office if he was powerless to prevent the publication of a question-
able statement, the usual answer was that "somebody else would
have been found" to authorize it. This may very well be true, but then
it also indicates the decisive fault of the system. Would somebody
else have also been found if the head of government would have had
to take the responsibility as the trustee of a powerful parliament?
(Weber, *Economy II*, p. 1438)

Weber deemed the struggle of the forces of freedom against
modern enslavement in the bonds of bureaucracy to be a battle of
sheer will against all odds. Individuality and freedom did not sail on
the favorable winds of history but had to fight hard to remain afloat
no matter how the economic tides changed. The "will" of a nation
and the determination of its political leaders determined the future
of freedom and individuality. Unlike Marx, Weber would not be
embarrassed if he were asked who the "We" of history is:

> Yet time is pressing: "we must work, while it is still day." If, in the
> course of succeeding generations, as long as the economic and intel-
> lectual "revolution," the much-abused "anarchy" of production and
> the no less abused "subjectivism" continue unabated, the individual
> citizen who through them, *and only through them*, has been left to
> depend on himself fails to conquer certain spheres of freedom and
> personality as his "inalienable" possessions, then he will *perhaps*
> never conquer them. (Weber, *Russia*, p. 283)

Prominently, the "We" of history for Weber is the politically active
intellectual who enters politics both with commitment to a cause
and with an awareness of the necessity of compromise in order to,
among other things, save the world from becoming the prison of
individuality and the graveyard of freedom.

An Ethic for Political Action

What may appear as a universal ethic for political action in Max
Weber's famous "Politics as a Vocation" is indeed one of the most
context-dependent of all his arguments. The narrow set of guidelines Weber offered for the practitioner of politics as a vocation was
inspired by an attempt to dispel the naiveté of politically motivated

intellectuals. It was also an attempt to prevent nihilism from setting in as a result of metatheoretical and theoretical assumptions that were taken for granted by most intellectuals of the day, and incidently by Weber himself. In this sense Weber's political essays, like his methodology, is a soliloquy. Weber argued that "some kind of faith must always exist. Otherwise . . . the curse of the creature's worthlessness overshadows even the externally strongest political successes" (Weber, *Politics*, p. 117). The recommendation of "ethics of responsibility," in other words, is novel and controversial only for the intellectuals; professional politicians to whom a "sense of proportion" and a lukewarm commitment to ideas come naturally will not be moved by this aspect of Weber's political creed.

Despite offering a nearly exhaustive list of possible forms of methodical political action, Weber remained critical of all of them. After all, his polytheistic social ontology was based on the ultimate irreconcilability of value spheres and the ineradicability of conflict from social life; assumptions that could hardly furnish a universal and ethically consistent political ethic. Indeed, Weber conceived of the relationship between spheres of ethics and politics as one of constant and unresolvable tension (Weber, *Rejections*, p. 333). Attempts at solving this tension, observed Weber, have time and again produced half-baked compromises, such as ethical rationalizations of political action, which Weber dubbed "aping of ethics," or the claims that success in action indicates moral right (Weber, *Politics*, p. 117; *Rejections*, p. 334). Such attempts appeared to Weber as full of unjustifiable compromises, and ultimately as being "dishonest" (Weber, *Rejections*, pp. 335-336). But in criticizing an "ethics of ultimate ends" Weber also took issue with apparently successful resolutions of the tension between ethical and rational (economic or political) action. A fairly inclusive taxonomy of political action oriented toward ultimate ends is offered in Weber's "Religious Rejections of the World and Their Directions." Unlike action that is "rational" from the "practical" point of view, the value of "ethically rational" action resides not in its success but in its "intrinsic worth." In other words, ethical action is by definition introverted. Nonetheless, those who opt to act publicly and politically according to value-rational frameworks—and Weber prefers that politicians at least to some extent do so—must keep an eye on the practical consequences of their action as well. Another problem aggravating the dilemma of ethically consistent political action is the necessity of using "violence" and manipulation of the "human machine" in order to achieve exalted ethical/political goals. Where religion supplies the ethics for political action Weber sees only two consistent ways out of this conundrum:

The puritan solution opts for inner-worldly asceticism. This means acting in the world according to a predetermined design and refusing to ponder the meaning of one's action or to take responsibility for its consequences. "The Christian does right and leaves the rest to God." When the action produces evil instead of good, the responsibility for it is passed on either to God himself or to the wickedness and foolishness of the creatural world, which might, at any rate, still be conceived of as "the best of all 'possible' worlds."

The second ethically consistent solution is not a "solution" of the problem as such, but a systematic avoidance of it. It consists of seeking refuge in otherworldly mysticism: the conflict of ethics and politics is thus avoided by completely retreating from the latter realm. This solution in its final logical form rejects categorically all forms of instrumentally rational action.

Less elaborate parallels for these alternatives of either retreating into the ivory tower of intellectual contemplation or engaging in a form of inner-worldly, noncontemplative asceticism abound in Eastern religions. Weber took particular interest in the Eastern brand of inner-worldly political asceticism and its unique justifications for entanglement in the world. A classical example of this type of solution appears in Bhagavad Gita. When Arjuna the master warrior fretted about endangering his salvation by performing his caste duties that included the killing of his kin, the supreme personality of godhead (Krishna) relieved him of his *angst* by declaring ethical concerns about one's actions to be invalid. Unable to perceive the pantheistic nature of the world (and social life), man is overcome by illusory appearances and their equally deceptive ethical meanings. Weber outlined the practical ethics implied here:

> Man of knowledge proves himself in action better against his own action in the world by consummating what is commanded—that always means caste duty—while inwardly remaining completely detached. That is he acts as if he acted not . . . as the early Christian "does right and leaves the rest to God" so the worshipper of the

Bahgavata does the "necessary work" . . . he does these and no
others without any concern for the consequences. (Weber, *India*, p. 184)

It is obvious that Weber considered none of these solutions for
the strain between ethics and politics as satisfactory. It is also clear
from our earlier sketch of Weber's theory of "social selection" that
the criterion of correctness of political action cannot be sought in
its external success either. Neither intellectuals' withdrawal from
the world nor their anarchistic pacifism nor their puritanical obsession with internal consistency and doing "the right thing" could
provide a guiding principle for political action from the point of
view of Weberian political ethics. Yet Weber was attracted to the
intellectualistic approach to politics. For instance, a measure of
ethical consistency in political action seems to have been significant
for Weber, as he often celebrated not only the internal consistency
and idealistic single-mindedness of certain types of political action
but also their usefulness: one can attain the possible only by wishing
the impossible. Besides, Weber knew that a rational choice between
an "ethics of ultimate ends" and an "ethics of responsibility" was
not possible and thus no final judgment between them could be
made (Weber, *Meaning*, p. 16). In an exceptionally revealing passage he goes so far as disclosing his basic partiality to the "ethics of
ultimate ends" when compared with the more "sober" and unenter-
prising political attitude of the bureaucratic intelligentsia:

In a sense, successful political action is always the "art of the possible." Nonetheless, the possible is often reached only by striving to
attain the impossible that lies beyond it. Those specific qualities of
our culture, which, despite our differences in viewpoint, we all es-
teem more or less positively, are not the products of the only consistent ethic of "'adaptation' to the possible," namely, the bureaucratic
morality of Confucianism. I, for my part, will not try to dissuade the
nation from the view that actions are to be judged not merely by their
instrumental value but by their intrinsic value as well. (Weber,
Meaning, pp. 23–24)

In addition, one must remember that Weber himself chose the
ethics of ultimate ends in respect to certain current political issues
of his time (Honigsheim, pp. 124–125). Even in "Politics as a Voca-

tion," one encounters passages such as the following: "Surely, politics is made with the head, but it is certainly not made with the head alone. In this the proponents of the ethics of ultimate ends are right" (Weber, *Politics*, p. 127). It is indeed this elective affinity of intellectuals for an ethic of ultimate ends that Weber finds in himself as well as in his audience that impels him to launch a fervent attack against this kind of political mentality.

Weber's critique of idealistic politics, however, was not designed to tacitly endorse the mundane practice of *realpolitik*. Professional politicians may not be impressed by Weber's emphasis on political "responsibility," but they too will benefit from his critique of power politics. "Politics as a Vocation" denounces the philistine attitude of power politicians and their utter neglect of the "tragedy with which all action, but especially political action, is truly interwoven" (Weber, *Politics*, p. 117). Considering the inevitability of the law of "unintended consequence" of human action—which becomes even more tragic as its dimensions are augmented in the sphere of political action—no one ought to take for granted the simple and rational purposive scheme of human action as appropriate for political action. The blatant insensitivity of professional power politicians to the Weberian paradoxes of political action generates more than scorn of the more realistic observers of human affairs; such neglect could foster serious practical problems as well. The arrogance of power politics can give rise to vainglory and conceit: by settling for the semblance of power these supposedly hardened practitioners of *realpolitik* would easily vitiate the purpose of their entering into politics by giving up the real power and settling for the vain semblances of power (Weber, *Politics*, pp. 116–117).

Turning his attention to intellectuals and their beloved "ethics of ultimate ends" in politics, Weber notes once more that "one cannot prescribe to anyone whether he or she should follow an ethic of absolute ends or an ethic of responsibility," but he proceeds to question the "inner poise"—and by implication the moral courage—of someone who opts for the ethics of ultimate ends, the easy solution of doing "the right thing," and then blaming the world for the consequences of the action. Acting "irresponsibly" and pretending to be blind to the consequences of one's own action is the sign of an immature and dilettante intellectual who willfully confuses the comforting vision of a rationally ordered world with the social reality that he attempts to influence by entering politics: "I am under the impression that in nine out of ten cases I deal with windbags who do not fully realize what they take upon themselves but who intoxicate themselves with romantic sensations" (Weber, *Politics*, p. 127). Here Weber explicitly casts doubt on the moral integrity of those who choose the ethics of ultimate ends as a dogmatic shield against the irrationality of the world and the perils of acting in it. The crusading pitch of Weber's "Politics as a Vocation" originates in his genuine hope of encouraging the intellectuals to enter politics while warning these natural followers of the ethics of ultimate ends against the dangers of political irresponsibility, especially when it comes seductively enveloped in such wrappings as anarchism and syndicalism. He censured the champions of the ethics of ultimate ends for their arrogance, for not being "human" or "mature" enough to give up the hope of fixing the world in their own image instead of adapting themselves to the demands of acting in the world as it stands. What is Weber's alternative? The "Ethics of Responsibility"! But what does that mean?

The basis of the ethics of responsibility is a simple inversion of the political attitude of the intellectuals: instead of the inward-looking quest for consistency and salvation through political action, they are advised to focus also on the consequences of their actions. They ought to face the utter irrationality of the world, the tragic results of the law of unintended consequences, the irreducible conflicts of value spheres, and, ultimately, they must abandon all hope to attain salvation through political action. Weber concluded that the crusader, religious and revolutionary alike, must learn that by entering politics he contracts with "diabolical forces." The intellectual entering politics must take responsibility not only for the consequences of his actions but also for "what may become of himself under the impact of these paradoxes" (Weber, *Politics*, pp. 120–126).

All of these caveats were intended for intellectuals who were considering a career in politics. One must remember that "Politics as a Vocation" was first delivered as a lecture to a group of students of politics. Weber was aware of the existence of radical students among his audience and that he had replaced another speaker (Kurt Eisner) who would have preached what Weber censored as ethics of ultimate ends in politics (Dahlmann, 1989). Weber could have concluded his lecture by simply recommending the supplantation of idealism with an ethic of responsibility. Weber did not do so because he was not sure that the ethics of ultimate ends was devoid of merit, and also because the alternative—the ethics of responsibility—which was already practiced by many nonintellectual politicians in any case, and which entailed a facile invitation to the time-honored virtues of temperance as moderation, did not appear to him as quite satisfactory.

Hence Weber reminded his audience once more of the unrationalizability of the world and the tragedy of having to act in it as though it were otherwise. We observed in the second chapter that the martial spirit has an elective affinity for polytheistic religiosity in Weber's sociology of religion. Conversely, we might conclude, acting courageously in a polytheistic world calls for the ethics of a hero; and this is Weber's final message to the intellectuals who contemplate acting in the world. Weber's most admirable political actor is neither a "cosmic ethical rationalist," nor a crusader in the cause of a clearly defined universal goal; and this is exactly why the actor needs to be a hero. It is not *because of* the meaningfulness of the world that the intellectual should enter public life and stand his ground, but *in spite of* its meaninglessness.

> Politics is a strong and slow boring of hard boards. It takes both passion and perspective. Certainly all historical experience confirms the truth—that man would not have attained the possible unless time and again he had reached out for the impossible. But to do that a man must be a leader, and not only a leader but a hero as well, in a very sober sense of the word. And even those who are neither leaders nor heroes must arm themselves with that steadfastness of heart which can brave even the crumbling of all hopes. This is necessary right now, or else men will not be able to attain even that which is possible today. Only he has the calling for politics who is sure that he shall not crumble when the world from his point of view is too stupid or too base for what he wants to offer. Only he who in the face of all this can say "In spite of all!" has the calling for politics. (Weber, *Politics*, p. 128)

4

Definitions

The Trouble with Defining Concepts

Waging a crusade against conceptual ambiguities is not an essential part of a social science based on Weberian principles. However, such a social science must not forswear formal considerations, because setting one's conceptual house in order might be inevitable in certain circumstances. The necessitating occasion may be a current of conceptual confusions or methodological controversies that threaten to interfere with the process of empirical investigation. For this reason Weber himself decided to write on the methodology of social and historical sciences. The subject of this book can especially benefit from formal delimitations and redefinitions because its central concepts have been subject to both scientific disputes and ideological feuds. Besides, an overhaul and reconstruction of the basic concepts of sociology of intellectuals is indispensable for one of the main purposes of this book: to further stimulate empirical research in the area of Weberian sociology of intellectuals. Of course, methodological considerations are not meant to supplant or guide empirical research. Ideal types, as we have already emphasized in the first chapter of this book, are simply "precision instruments." They are modest tools; so modest indeed that they do not even require to be inspected for their truth or falsehood but rather for the degree of their usefulness. The set of interrelated ideal types offered here (Table 4.1–4.3) is meant to be of pragmatic use for the practitioners of a Weberian sociology of intellectuals. As such the chief virtue of the model offered in this chapter and amplified in successive cross tables is not its novelty but its inclusiveness; it synthesizes elements of two kinds of diversity: that of theoretical debates aiming to define intellectuals, and the divergence of the historical and intercivilizational varieties of intellectuality.

At the outset it must be pointed out that the apparent "generalizations" on which our model is based are not inductively constructed; concepts such as intellectuals, intelligentsia, and men and women of knowledge are heuristic devices. For one thing these concepts do not claim to represent ontologically significant and universal phenomena. Rather, they prominently bear the imprint of particular historical and geocultural "value-relevant interests" of Western civilization.

Being temporally and geoculturally grounded does not necessarily vitiate the purpose of these concepts, which is to compare and contrast different civilizations. Nor is the claim to universality by such ideal types tantamount to an imperialistic attempt to monopolize the science of intercultural understanding. The Weberian discipline is consistent with the proposition that more than one set of "universally valid" ideal types can be constructed and used for intercivilizational comparisons. In other words, a Weberian social science allows for each generation and each civilization to construct its own universally valid ideal types on the basis of its own value-relevant interests. The recognition of the relevance of limited human interests in the process of concept formation has a direct bearing on the problems surrounding the general "definition" of the concepts with which we are dealing in this chapter.

Some of the best studies of intellectuals shrink from offering a "definition" for intellectuals in order to shun premature closures or to avoid an earlier period's parochial and Eurocentric generalizations that often stretched a concept beyond its legitimate Western context and thus beyond its usefulness. We need not fear this as long as we are aware of our position in time and space and the conceptual limits our "human condition" sets on us. It is with this knowledge that we heuristically apply a battery of context-dependent concepts to temporally and geoculturally distant peoples. If done correctly, this exploration will allow us to "understand" them in a way that is both scientific and humane.

When engaging in this type of heuristic analysis we must expect rhetorical questions that betray a confusion between Weberian cross-cultural references and the boorish and protoscientific anthropology and historiography of an earlier period of Western scholarship. We will be asked: How could you possibly lump together the Greek sophists, the Confucian mandarins, the medieval monks, and the Islamic scribes under such rubrics as "intellectuals" or "intelligentsia," which were after all developed in nineteenth-century France and Russia?[1] The answer is that we can, only if we are aware of the similarities and differences between these very different types. Civilizational perspectives are legitimate grounds for concept formation. This statement applies to all civilizations equally; we recognize the right of those civilizations that are the object of our scientific investigations to return the gaze of understanding in their own terms; they can legitimately call our intellectuals "scribes," or "mandarins," if this usage is a judicious one and if it helps them to thereby achieve a better intercultural "understanding." In the course of this book we have provided many examples of Weber's use of exclusively Western concepts in discussing phenomena of Indian, Chinese, and Hebrew civilizations, but examples of this type of intercivilizational reference, heuristic, ironic or otherwise, abound everywhere. Take for instance, Simone de Beauvoir's choice of the title *Mandarins*, for a novel about a group of radical French intellectuals. Only a pedant will take such a reference literally. In ways that are not entirely dissimilar to the ironic use of cross-civilizational references, every time we use the concept of "intellectual" for phenomena pertaining to a time and place other than that of their origin, we must expect our audience to look beyond the literal usage.

Only if we take pains to compare and contrast distant civilizational types can we discover similarities beneath apparent differences. Diverse types of intellectuals share many common features. They all are the beneficiaries of a system of division of labor that allows them to engage in the process of formal and substantive rationalization of ideas. They all foster internal hierarchies and relate to the hierarchies of prestige and power in their societies in a limited number of ways. Intellectuals everywhere are responsible for cultural borrowings or resistance to civilizational osmoses. They are largely responsible for the unique flavor of different cultures. That the Athenians looked to Sparta or Persia for guidance, and that the Israelites deliberately avoided importing the intellectual products of their neighbors or even guest cultures (Egyptians, Babylonians, and Syrians) is to a great extent due to the predilections of the intellectual strata in these cultures. A sociology of intellectuals, and indeed any kind of sociology, must undertake the risk of comparing what might appear to be cultural dissimilarities to attain comparative insights and to study counterfactual trends in the civilizational developments. Thus we have explored an array of striking similarities between ideologies and counterideologies of intellectuals in a cross section of diverse civilizational contexts (see Appendix C).

The fear of general concepts (well founded as it might be in the case of certain kinds of careless theorizing that have occasionally passed as sociology) often leads to a form of sterile and snobbish empirical puritanism, which Weber opposed in his arguments against German historiographers: the objective reality is too rich to be studied in its entirety. We need conceptual sieves to sift through empirical data and to scientifically reduce the empirical reality to a manageable size. That these conceptual sieves are crafted in our cultures and bear the insignia of our rootedness in time and space must concern us only if we are not aware of such biases or if we embark on a quixotic attempt to disavow our particularity. As mortals we are bound to a tiny slice of time and space, and Weber (before Gadamer and his *Hermeneutics*) urged us to face this condition both in considering the calling to engage in "Science as a Vocation" as well as in the way we engage in it. Once we are aware of our "limitedness" we can turn it into "perspective," an intercultural "Archimedean point" that alone lets us understand the other. Mutual intercultural (or historical) understanding does not require a single universal set of scientific theories but several ones. We understand the other (i.e., the historically or geoculturally distant peoples) not despite our particularity but because of it.

In creating a new taxonomy of the usages of the concept of "intellectuals" and "intelligentsia" we have resisted the temptation to coin new words for fear of contributing to the methodological confusions. Instead of designating one usage as correct and dismissing the rest, our proposed cross tabulation (Tables 4.1 and 4.2) reproduces the common overlapping usages that have resulted in many confusions. Thus the concept "Intellectuals" appears twice in our model: once in vertical order (as opposed to vast numbers of "Intelligentsia") and then again in horizontal order (in contrast to

TABLE 4.1. Cross-Tabulation of the Types (Mission/Calling) and Layers (Intellectuals/Intelligentsia): Functions

	Masses ——→ Meaning	Masses ←——→ Meaning
TYPES OF COMMITMENT: to masses or the truth	SEEKERS OF PURE KNOWLEDGE: MEN/WOMEN OF SCIENCE/ ARTS/LETTERS	COMMITTED INTELLECTUALS: LIBERATORS, SAVIORS, "ENGAGE" THINKERS
LAYERS: Varieties of reason & hierarchies	Committed to "*meaning*" (truth, beauty, gnosis, knowledge overarching structures, etc.) They have a "*calling*."	Committed to "*masses*" (lead, reform, liberate, save, bring "happiness," etc.) They have a "*mission*."
INTELLECTUALS: (Theoretical reason, "intellect") creative, heretic, or prophetic	**1** Rationalization of ideas by: DEVOTEES OF PURE TRUTH	**2** Reinterpretation of ideas by: LEADING REFORMERS AND REVOLUTIONARIES
INTELLIGENTSIA: (Practical reason, "intelligence") organizer, interpreter, keeper	**3** Reinterpretation and routinization of ideas by: KEEPERS OF TRADITION	**4** Application of ideas by: PRACTICAL AGENTS OF IDEAS

TABLE 4.2. Cross-Tabulation of the Types (Mission/Calling) and Layers (Intellectuals/Intelligentsia): Positions and Professions

TYPES OF COMMITMENT: to masses or the truth *LAYERS:* Varieties of reason & hierarchies	SEEKERS OF PURE KNOWLEDGE: MEN/WOMEN OF SCIENCE/LETTERS/ARTS Committed to *"meaning"* (truth, beauty, gnosis, knowledge overarching structures, etc.) They have a *"calling."* *Masses ——→ Meaning*			COMMITTED INTELLECTUALS: LEADERS, LIBERATORS, SAVIORS Committed to *"masses"* (lead, reform, liberate, save, bring "happiness," etc.) They have a *"mission."* *Masses ←—— Meaning*		
	Science	Religion	Thought	Science	Religion	Thought
INTELLECTUALS: (Theoretical reason, "intellect") creative, heretic, or prophetic	Top scientist, discoverer	Exemplary prophet	Top theorist	Major inventor	Emissary prophet	Reformer, revolutionary philosopher/king
INTELLIGENTSIA: (Practical reason, "intelligence") organizer, interpreter, keeper	Expert, researcher	Theologian monk, mystic	Scholar, critic	Engineer doctor, lawyer, teacher	Priest, mentor, scribe, teacher	Agitator, activist, bureaucrat, teacher, mass media, publishing

seekers of pure knowledge: "scientists/writers/artists etc."). The model amplifies the confusion in the usage of the term "Intellectual" before reordering its elements and resolving the confusion. The model could be viewed as asking the "native": When you say "Intellectuals" do you mean as opposed to top "scientists/writers/artists" or do you mean as opposed to "Intelligentsia"?

Another purpose of the present model is to include almost all types and professions that have been identified with intellectuals and intelligentsia, preserving for the empirical researcher the prerogative of excluding a particular category in any given research project. The above cross-tabulation is based on Weber's theory of the relative autonomy of the sphere of ideas as it also reflects his interest in the interface of ideas and interests.

The Horizontal Differentiation

The horizontal axis differentiates intellectuals on the basis of their commitment to "ideas" on one extreme and to "the people" on the other. Intellectuals share the lonely journey of "Men and Women of Letters / Science / Art (that lead away from the people) to transcend the banality of quotidian existence. They all aspire to attain a higher state of universal bliss, to attain Sophia, Gnosis, Knowledge, Truth, Beauty, Overall Patterns and Structures, and in short, the "Meaning" and the "Essence" of life. Many of the definitions of men and women of knowledge and "Intellectuals" focus on the means and consequences of this search, namely, the heavy and dense use of symbols and the creation of a privatized jargon that often turn into passwords to privileged inner circles or even into symbolic tools of power and domination. But these are all either means or consequences of the original quest for meaning that alone signifies both intellectuals and seekers of pure knowledge. The two groups are fellow travelers on the road to transcendence. Intellectuals are born once some decide to "come back" to the masses with the fruits of their discoveries. This differentiation is therefore primarily based on a moral choice rather than on a hierarchy of more or less talented. While seekers of pure knowledge have a "calling" to pursue the truth, intellectuals are committed to a "mission" to return to the masses. Classical Greek "intellectuals" debated whether "The Good Life" consisted in the life of the intellect or in public life in the *polis*. Plato was certain that it lay in intellectual life, but he also argued that the philosopher who had acquired a taste for basking in the sun of truth and beauty (who would naturally be loath to go back to the dark and dank cave of ordinary people in order to lead them) ought nevertheless to go back. At the two poles of this allegorical movement between the truth and the masses we can discern the archetypical categories of philosophers and philosopher-kings.

We have already observed an elective affinity between the development of an "ideology of intellectuals," that is, a theory advocating the political empowerment of intellectuals, and the belief in the three principles of (1) the existence of truth, (2) its attainability and social relevance, and (3) the assumption that intellectuals would selflessly carry out the search for truth. The "counterideologies" of intellectuals usually attack the last two premises (attainability and social relevance of truth, and particularly, the alleged selflessness of its carriers). We have also pointed out that an elective affinity exists between the view of historical progress as a "semiautomatic" machination (advocated by Auguste Comte, Lester F. Ward, V. I. Lenin, and George Lukacs and most of the reformist thinkers) and the ideology of intellectuals who would then take the wheel and steer history in the right direction. By contrast, the "fully automatic" evolution (advocated by Herbert Spencer, William G. Sumner, Bakunin, Rosa Luxemburg, and most of the anarchist, libertarian, and conservative thinkers) has been favored by the counterideologies of intellectuals for its implication that history has no need for the meddling of some complacent savants professing to correct its course.[2]

The flow of converts between the two categories of intellectuals and seekers of pure knowledge (regions 1 and 2) depends on historical circumstances. Whenever there is a coherent and compelling ideology of intellectuals, or whenever there is a definite social cause or an indisputable "good," seekers of pure knowledge are likely to consider seriously that, besides responding to their calling to pursue the truth, they must also fulfill their duty to a social "mission"; to turn toward the people whom they had left in the cave of quotidian illusions; to become "intellectuals." As a rule, however, seekers of pure knowledge encounter this alleged mission with trepidation: from the point of view of enthusiasts of knowledge, intellectuals are in danger of compromising their integrity and willingly engage in what Weber called "the sacrifice of intellect." Conversely, periods of great social upheaval caused or exacerbated by intellectuals, and especially disastrous failures of reformist movements, bring in their wake mass defections of socially committed intellectuals to the ranks of seekers of pure knowledge (from region 2 to region 1). As a matter of course, however, seekers of knowledge who neglect their social mission by carrying on their quest for truth must appear to intellectuals as a selfish and elitist caste, wistfully indulging their eccentric hobbies at the expense of their people.

The variety of arguments between intellectuals (seekers of knowledge) and (scientists/writers/artists) represents a great deal of literature written about intellectuals, by intellectuals, and for—or against—intellectuals. Plato urged the *polis* to force the contemplative intellectuals to come back to the cave of everyday illusions and undertake the putatively unpleasant task of leading the people. He also advised against tolerating those intellectuals who refuse to think in a responsible or constructive way; poets among others were to be banished from his Republic. Marx predicted that a group of intellectuals would join the people (working class) but not before seeing that the end of their class privileges was at hand. An excellent example of this debate can be found in the public exchange that kept Sartre and Camus at loggerheads over the "responsibility" of intellectuals to join the public protests against the French war in Algeria. Those contemplative intellectuals who recognize their social "mission" do not necessarily remain in their own sub-category in transition from region 1 to region 2. A scientist, for instance, does not always turn into an inventor (see Table 4.2). Contemporary scientists (e.g., Sakharov) and philosophers (e.g., Russell or Sartre) often advocated political positions totally unrelated to their field of research. Consistent with the platonic scenario, the charisma emanating from having been closer to the source of normative philosophical or scientific truths seems to have sufficiently legitimized the political ambitions of intellectuals.

Max Weber did not merely sanction this kind of engagement. He went out of his way to encourage intellectuals' direct participation in political processes, because he feared the coming hegemony of the bureaucratic intelligentsia. But Weber, as we have demonstrated in Chapter 3, was also weary of intellectuals' political naiveté, dogmatism, and irresponsibility. This feeling led him to go to great lengths to warn intellectuals against the perils of confusing the attitude called for in the symmetrical and consistent universe of intellectuality and that they needed to adopt once they chose "Politics as a Vocation." An interesting reaction to the dilemma of the seekers of pure knowledge wishing to preserve their integrity while engaging in politics can be discerned in George Orwell's advice to intellectuals who wish to fulfill their social "mission" without compromising their commitments to the pursuit of truth: "When a writer engages in politics he should do so as a citizen, as a human being, not *as a writer* . . . should he refrain from writing *about* politics? . . . certainly not! . . . Only he should do so as an individual, as outsider, at the most as unwelcome guerrilla on the flank of a regular army" (Orwell, 1960, pp. 270–271).

Before turning to the vertical differentiation of intellectuals and intelligentsia let us consider a probable criticism that might be leveled against our definition of seekers of pure knowledge as seekers of some kind of universal truth. This definition may be said not to fit the postmodern intellectual. In response, first let us remember that doubts, cynicism, and even hostility to the ideals of universal or objective truth and beauty or their purity or attainability are so old as to be virtually coterminous with the birth of intellectuality. Any reader of Greek classics knows that to argue that "truth" is nothing but power in disguise, or that it is but a semantic illusion is not an altogether novel invention of poststructuralism. From the sociological point of view, however, the carriers of such ideas, regardless of the content of their message, are easily categorized as intellectuals. They are to be identified as intellectuals not only because of their social function and way of life (e.g., livelihood, language, etc.) but also because the search for transcending the illusions (including that of truth and beauty) is a singularly intellectual one. This search too involves a "journey" leading to an alleged higher state of awareness assumed by the critic, a feeling of liberation not only from the simple-minded delusions of the common folk but also from the vulgarity of less sophisticated colleagues. The distance thus created between traditional, modern, or postmodern intellectuals and the naive duration of everyday experience is signified—now as much as ever—by jargon, a careful and critical mode of speech, a privatized language that Gouldner, following Bernstine, has called the "Culture of Critical Discourse."

The important criterion for our horizontal differentiation is that both seekers of pure knowledge and intellectuals, through contemplation and discourse, do, to varying extents, "depart" from the quotidian reality of everyday life; whether they achieve their "nirvana" is of secondary importance. Our ideal typical model thus seems to remain relevant as long as unforeseeable substantive changes in the tradition of Western intellectuality have not dissolved all interest in contemplation and discourse, or as long as a Tolstoyesque mood of populism has not caused mass defections from the intellectual and contemplative way of life by which we identify the intellectuals.

Having said this, we must also concede the seminal importance of the substantive changes in modern occidental art and intellectuality. As with almost every other aspect of the so-called postmodern development, the occidental revolt against the occidental "logos" was already present in what is generally known as "Modernism." Weber addressed the issues of "disenchantment of the world," and the indulging of intellectuals in the irrational cores of life, (e.g., in eros). As the great theorist of the avant-garde, Renato Poggioli, has pointed out, the movement in modern art away from rational perspective, proportion, representation, and humanism toward the portrayal of the grotesque, the novel, the non-Western, the mechanistic, the abstract, and the surrealistic was already present in the art of the turn of the century. At that time, artists replaced rational and purposive execution—reasoned "action" with which social scientists deal—with "gesture" and spontaneous techniques. In his article under the heading "Intellectuals" in the *Encyclopedia of Social Sciences*, Edward Shils has rightly discussed these new movements not as a series of breaks with intellectuality but as its secondary traditions.

The movement away from Western reason, which has been praised by a section of leading contemporary intellectuals as ground breaking, had already been recognized by Weber and hailed by Marcuse and Adorno as the only avenue of salvation from the reified formal reason that has come to dominate the modern Occident. The current vogue of postmodern literary criticism is but a continuation of what has already happened in the world of art and architecture without truly disrupting the continuation of the Western bourgeoisie and its economic and political systems. For all their obstreperous rebelliousness, the oppositional movements of this century are possible only in the bosom of bourgeois society, which they continue to decry. The history of this century has shown that antirational movements quickly wither away even at the helm of the very alternatives they seek (e.g., fascism and socialism). In any case, the artist, the scholar, and the intellectual still (and perhaps more than ever) *depart* from everyday life by a disciplined and adept use of language and symbols in search of a kind of "truth," even if it is to proclaim that there is no such thing. Schumpeter's theory that capitalism cannot fight the oppositional intellectual because it is based on freedom of commerce is somewhat eccentric. Weber has convincingly demonstrated that the kind of liberty Schumpeter alludes to is no longer necessary for fully mature capitalism. To discover reasons for tolerating oppositional intellectuals in the West we must look in the direction of the "relatively autonomous" sphere of politically liberal ideals that the Western world has institutionalized and sacralized. These ideals will remain effective, however, only as long as the Western "people" do not abandon them. Unlike Schumpeter, Weber did not take these guarantees of liberty for granted.

The Vertical Differentiation

Our vertical classification in the tables must be more familiar to the sociologically trained reader. Rather than depending on a voluntaristic choice between serving the people or seeking the truth, it is based on a more objective ranking order. In the *top category* are placed the intellectuals, the best and the brightest, the "producers" of intellectual commodities; on the *lower level* are located the humble processors, the mediocre "consumers" and disseminators of thought products. Of course, it is not entirely true that the group at the bottom does not create, nor that to belong to one or the other is purely a matter of objective criteria of excellence. Even here a "choice" must be made between Weber's "theoretical" and "practical" reason, between what ancient Greeks alternatively called *sophia* and *phrenosis*, or between what Richard Hofstadter (1962) has labeled "intellect" and "intelligence." However, the way this choice is made depends as much on the intellectual talents and qualifications of the agent as it does on the agent's ideal propensities.

The interest of the historical and sociological approaches in the vertical classification is due to its hierarchical nature and to the huge numbers of intelligentsia that form its base. Perhaps another reason for the popularity of the category of intelligentsia is that it is more sociologically tangible. By this we mean that a stratum of intelligentsia resembles the rest of the strata and classes in society in the unproblematic way in which it organizes and embraces an array of ideas to protect its interests. Unlike intellectuals whose ideal interest in rational development of ideas clashes with any fixed ideological arrangement of them, the intelligentsia naturally advocate ideas that are conducive to its class or status interests. It is not surprising therefore to see that the major attention of the sociology of intellectuals has been focused on intelligentsia. The majority of the literature in the Marxist theory of intellectuals also has dealt with intelligentsia. Gouldner's criticism of Marxist literature (that it is ventriloquist and unreflexive, that it does not account for itself in the same language in which it talks about creation of ideas and ideologies among other classes) can be interpreted as criticizing the absence of intellectuals from the Marxist sociology of intelligentsia. The most cogent theory of intellectuals in the Marxist discourse is that of Gramsci (1978). Yet he, too, seems to be talking about intelligentsia when he asserts that everyone in the society is to some extent an intellectual and that all classes have their own "organic intellectuals." Any class analysis of ideas cannot help but expand the sociology of intelligentsia.

Conversely, any sociology of intellectuals that wishes to focus on "intellectuals" in the sense we have defined the term in the vertical differentiation tends to transcend class barriers. Mannheim's notion of the "free-floating intellectual" is a case in point. This theoretical strand within the sociology of intellectuals is based on the observation that the category of "intellectuals" comprises a small number of creative individuals. The thin stratum of intellectuals is not merely the object of external conflicts with the laity, the authorities, and the intelligentsia. It also harbors a profound inner tension between its own ideal and material interests. How can such a group be conceived of as an ideologically ambitious class? Intellectuals' "ideal interests" lie in the constant rationalization of the sphere of ideas and in a relentless attempt to transcend the immediate world in search of its meaning, its essence, or its beauty. Ideas that emanate from this search can only occasionally be conducive to the interests of various social classes and strata. Viewed as a flux, ideas are destabilizing and potentially dangerous to the interests of any given social class, including those of the intellectuals themselves. To recapitulate: stable ideal edifices cannot be built on the lava flow of ideas. Intellectuals are by definition unstable as a class because, as the carriers of relatively autonomous ideas, they cannot abide for long a moratorium on thinking critically about any set of sacred ideas, even when such ideas tend to justify their own material interests.

Society's fear of the constant rationalizing process that would erode its "core ideas" has given rise to a distrust of intellectuals, who are the carriers of, this process, to their feelings of "alienation," and finally, to an array of objective social sanctions against intellectuals. These sanctions are usually devised and enforced by a nucleus of anti-intellectual ex-intellectuals who have already performed the "sacrifice of intellect." In the religious sphere this is exemplified as the church's establishment of official limits on freewheeling thinking by creating "dogma." Conforming to dogma is less a source of painful soul-searching for intelligentsia than it is for intellectuals; because the former have less vested (ideal) interest in unadulterated rationalizations of ideas or pure thinking.

Max Weber's political sociology highlights the potential tension inherent in the vertical differentiation of intellectuals and intelligentsia. In the third chapter we have referred to Weber's fear that the subservience of intelligentsia to their own interests as well as to other social interests would make them perfect superintendents for what he termed the "iron cage" or the "house of bondage" of the future. His observations about socioeconomic forces of modernity combined with his study of ancient oriental bureaucracies had provided Weber with a daunting insight about the irreversible bureaucratizing trends of the modern society, which would guarantee the further entrenchment of a proliferating intelligentsia at the expense of the increasing isolation of intellectuals. He foresaw the possibility of "orientalization" of the West: organized state bureaucracies would control masses of postmodern "fellahin." Thus Weber staked his hopes on individualistic intellectuals to fight the tide of the grim future and its bureaucratic storm troopers: the intelligentsia.

It is tempting to compare the difference between intellectuals and intelligentsia with Weber's distinction between those who live "for" politics and those who live "off" of it. Indeed, Weber makes this distinction in the context of contrasting the political intellectuals who enter politics with a mission, on the one hand, and the career-ism of party intelligentsia, on the other. The former live "for" political ideals and the latter live "off" them. This point demon-strates the consistency of the ideal types proposed in this chapter and the ideal types of Weber. But it will also show us how these ideal types must *not* be used. These ideal types are only of analytical value. As such they are meant only for the indirect use of the empirical researcher. Those who live for politics also, and quite frequently, live off it as well (Weber, *Politics*, p. 84). In a similar manner our definition of an "intellectual" can be exclusively ap-plied only in limited cases to a given individual or stratum. Only in so far as one engages in a particular kind of reasoning is one a man of woman of knowledge, science, letters, or arts. Only in so far as this person turns back to bring a Promethean gift for the masses is he or she an intellectual. At other moments the same person could be a member of intelligentsia, for instance when he or she attends a trade union meeting of artists, writers, or university professors. Of course, as there are people who enter different categories depending on historical changes, the period of their life and even time of day, there are those who readily conform to the pure type and can be safely placed in a category. A rarely reflective specialist, a typical bureaucrat, a scientist, or a philosopher totally dedicated to the discovery of truth can rest in any of the square abodes on the diagonal apposite ends of our cross-tabulation (Table 4.2). The validity of our cross tabulation, however, does not depend on their numbers, or even on their existence.

Columns and Rows

One of the interesting properties of the cross tabulation of Table 4.2 is the capacity of its columns and rows to reflect the varieties of controversies that have characterized the debate between intellectuals (in both senses,), seekers of pure knowledge, and the intelligentsia. We can slightly alter our cross tables (Tables 4.1 and 4.2) to fashion an instrument for classifying the varieties of debates that have occurred within the sphere of intellectuality (Table 4.3). The first column in this table could be said to represent the otherworldly orientation of intellect—as the "departure" from the life world of the masses indicated in the previous two tables. The second column represents the inner-worldly orientation of intellectuals in the same sense that a "return to the masses" charcterized them in the previous tables. The rows represent the hierarchy of intellectuals and intelligentsia, as well as their respective affinity for theoretical or practical reason. In the first column we can locate such works of literature as Dostoyevsky's "Grand Inquisitor" chapter in *Brothers Karamazov* where a priest confronts Jesus, whose Second Coming cannot help but undo the stability of the church. Weber's frequent references to the tensions between prophets and priests may also be seen as a typical tension between the top and bottom sections of the first column. Florian Znaniecki in his seminal work, *The Social Role of the Man of Knowledge* (1965), also describes the relationship between the top and the bottom of the first column: Znaniecki's "The Discoverer of Truth" would be placed at the top of the first column while "The Systematizer" belongs at the bottom. The unification of the two roles, however, occasionally occurs; that is, a discoverer of truth might actually found his or her own school of thought. Znaniecki's metaphor is also one of movement and is consistent with the simile we have used in the horizontal differentiation: the seeker of pure knowledge is "going," he or she is facing the truth. To become an intellectual one must *turn back* (toward the people); to become a member of intelligentsia (a systematizer) one must *stop*. A seeker of pure knowledge who "wants to found a school must know when to stop in his or her function, *Principia non sunt multiplicanda praeter necessitatem*" (Znaniecki, 1965, p. 123)

The relationships between revolutionaries and party functionaries and those between politicians and state bureaucrats typify the tensions between the top and the bottom of the second column. The controversy between Lenin and Luxemburg is an example of this debate.

The literature describing the "choice" between the first row (otherworldly calling) and second row (inner-worldly mission) has also produced a great deal of literature. At the top of the intellectual hierarchy we can place works such as Weber's "Politics as a Vocation," and at the lower row we might consider works debating the relative merits of various intellectual occupations, such as a sixth-century document by a Persian philosopher who is discussing whether to become a philosopher, a religious leader, or a physician, and after careful consideration he decides to choose the latter (Baabe Borzouyeh Tabib) (Table 4.2).

It goes without saying that certain areas of our original cross tabulation (Tables 4.1–4.3) present more complications than others. Regions 1 and 4 are the simplest, as they represent more simple and monolithic elements: the realm of ideas (region 1) that is, the logical and cumulative rationalizing trends of pure ideas, can be best carried on unencumbered by the concerns of this world. Similarly, region 4 is relatively simple, as it represents the intersection of practical reason, and of inner-wordly zeal for applying the revealed or discovered principles.

Regions 2 and 3 are the most complicated, as they tend to combine in varying proportions a melange of less compatible elements.

TABLE 4.3. Cross-Tabulation of the Primacy of Calling or Mission of Intellectuals and Their Role as Carriers or Organizers of Ideas: Literature

	Seekers of pure knowledge (otherworldly)				Committed intellectuals (inner-worldly)		
	1				**2**		
Intellectuals as carriers of ideas		*		"Politics as a vocation"		*	
				* ———————— *			
		"G	I			"W	B
		r	n			h	e
		a	q			a	
		n	u			t	D
	3	d	i		**4**		o
Intelligentsia as organizers of ideas			s			I	n
			i			s	e?"
			t				
			o	"Babe Borzouyeh Tabib"		T	
			r"	* ———————— *		o	

Region 2, for instance combines abstract maxims derived from pure ideas with an inner-worldly zeal for their actualization. Emissary prophecy, leading a revolution, or being a philosopher-king all involve a more complicated synthesis of elements than anything that can be found in the first region. A monk, a scholar, and a researcher, whom we classify in region 3, have to balance their otherwordly aspirations with the demands of their position in society, which may not accommodate them as well as it does their sources of emulation in region 1.

The cross tabulations offered in this chapter may also be used to create a taxonomy of the types of more recent empirical and theoretical works done in the field of sociology of intellectuals. Many of the empirical works suffer from insufficient clarity of definition. Others seem to subscribe to mutually exclusive definitions. Using the cross tabulations proposed here will allow the admission of almost all of these works to a unified and cumulative body of sociology of intellectuals. Konrad and Szelenyi (1979), Djilas (*The New Class*), and the majority of Eastern European scholars deal with the lower row (regions 3 and 4) as well as with transition of, and contradiction between, the intellectuals of region 2 and the intelligentsia of region 4. As a rule those with an interest in the class position of intellectuals usually focus on the intelligentsia of the bottom row. The exception to this rule would be the conspiratorial theories of anarchists and certain extreme forms of populism or even Marxism that worry about a takeover of the society by a band of Jacobin intellectuals (e.g., Bakunin and Machajski).

The idealist tradition from Plato to Durkheim and Parsons focuses, however though not exclusively, on the upper half of the table. In this group we also categorize those who prefer to underline the dissent: the destabilizing and oppositional properties of intellectuals such as Feuer and Dahrendorf and even Shils. From our point of view the decision either to support or to oppose the existing order is one that is made by the intellectuals in an extraintellectual realm of values. Ideas that lend themselves to such positions, however, are produced in the same region of intersection of theoretical reason and inner-worldly concerns. Opposition, alienation and censure can be caused by the transnational character of the rationalizing process, by the desire of intellectuals to tamper with the "core ideas," "noble lies," and sacred values of the society. However, it can also be caused by a theoretically consistent adherence to the core values of the society, while the actual constellation of interests of dominant groups favors neglecting their authentic form in favor of compromises. When this happens intellectuals are alienated and prosecuted as a new orthodoxy, not for opposing the core values but for their unadulterated loyalty to them. Most of the works about American intellectuals that concentrate on their alienation, marginality, and opposition, including the recent interest in New York intellectuals represented by Alan Wald (1987) and Thomas Bender (1987), can be categorized in this section.

Russell Jacoby's *The Last Intellectuals* (1987) addresses an ominous development in what he defines as the disappearance of intellectuals in academia. He is talking of a massive shift from the right column (regions 2 and 4) to the left column (regions 1 and 3).

Weber's "politics as a vocation" addresses problems that arise when seekers of pure knowledge enter the sphere of politics (from region 1 to region 2) but refuse to tone down the ethics of ultimate ends, which is a survival of their pervalent ethos in a world of pure thought. This essay also deals with intellectuals' objective conflict with the bureaucracies that would be placed under them in the second column.

Besides categorizing the already existing research, one can envision the possibility of conducting new intercivilizational research in the area of Weberian sociology of intellectuals. For instance, the intercivilizational study of religious intelligentsia can benefit from the section of our model that deals with the religious intellectuality (Table 4.4). Both the Buddhist and the Islamic concepts allow the

TABLE 4.4. Comparative Study of Religious Intellectuality
in Islam and Buddhism

	Departure for the Holy	*Return for Saving Others*
Leaders	1. EXEMPLARY PROPHECY Islam: Vali Buddhism: Buddha	2. EMISSARY PROPHECY Islam: Nabi Buddhism: Buddhisatva
Followers	3. MYSTIC QUEST, monk Islam: Aref Buddhism: Monk	4. CURE OF SOULS, priest Islam: Alem Buddhism: —

leader a spiritual as well as physical departure from people and the reality of everyday life in order to attain the spiritual truth, they also demand a selfless return, in order to bring salvation to the denizens of the mundane world. It is very difficult to locate substantive similarities between the "truths" sought in the two religious traditions, yet our model facilitates a comparison between the types of religious intellectuals and intelligentsia in so far as they emulate their leaders in "departing" from and "returning" to the people. The exemplary prophecy of Buddhism has an emissary aspect as the emissary prophecy of Islam has an exemplary root. Both Islam and Buddhism allow a following for the pure seeker of truth or the exemplary prophet, the Buddhist monk and the Islamic mystic (Sufi or Aref), although this position is much more central to Buddhism than it is to Islam. But, Buddhism lacks the institution of priesthood. We must note that none of these statements can be illuminating without qualifications that must highlight the reasons that the comparison holds the the extent to which it does not.

Appendix A

Weber on the "Positivist–Intuitionist" Controversy

To shield themselves from the positivist onslaught, some social thinkers[1] took it upon themselves to erect a "Chinese wall" between the realms of "nature" and "culture." To further protect themselves, they turned the latter into the magical garden of "subjectifying" sciences (Weber, *Knies*, p. 130) at whose gates the laws of causality stopped (Weber, *Knies*, p. 135). The trodden paths of natural determination and empirical observation within this domain trailed off into the mist of "human freedom." The alleged unpredictability of human action was perceived as neither a disadvantage nor, as their kinder adversaries maintained, as a sign of the youth of the cultural sciences. On the contrary, it signified the dignity of the realm of the humanities and had to be treasured as such. The depth of this mysterious realm could be fathomed only in the light of "empathetic understanding," "suggestive 'interpretation,'" "feelings of totality," and the like (Weber, *Knies*, p. 177).

If Weber seems to disenchant this magical garden it is not because he is willing to give ground to positivist reductionism. In fact, Weber, being an advocate of *verstehen*, felt comfortable doing away with the magic of subjectivity because he did not need to hide behind it. This was so because he never took the monopolistic pretensions of positivism to the realm of science seriously. Weber was able to transcend the positivist-intuitionist controversy, and in doing so, he once more leaped ahead of his time, anticipating the latest turns in the sociology of science. Consider the following.

> Even the knowledge of the most certain proposition of our theoretical sciences—e.g., the exact natural sciences or mathematics, is, like the cultivation and refinement of the conscience, a product of culture. (Weber, *Objectivity*, p. 55)

Nevertheless, if one wants to imagine Weber as a defender of the autonomy of the cultural sciences in the face of positivist invasion, one might characterize his strategies as uniquely offensive. Note that, for example, in the case of "unpredictability" of human action, Weber neither establishes it as a weakness of the social sciences to be overcome by further development of these disciplines, nor does he glorify it as a unique property of the humanities to be cultivated and recognized as such. Instead, he points out that this situation arises because the historical and sociocultural phenomena are important for us as individual events. And individual events by definition cannot be deduced from general laws, as none of the nomological formulas of mechanics can predict the way a specific falling rock would break into splinters (Weber, *Knies*, p. 122). But this does not usually pose a problem for natural sciences because they are, in the majority of cases, interested in generalized statements about the laws governing "nature,"[2] which is for Weber a logically (not empirically, as positivists presumed) closed system (Parsons, 1964, pp. 8–9). When this is not the case (e.g., in the case of seismology and meteorology), insofar as the empirical disciplines in question are interested in specific predictions rather than the general laws governing change in nature, they are also faced with the problem of unpredictability.

Or, take the "lawmaking" controversy. Here, too, Weber's position is based upon exposing the weaknesses of the positivist argument. This renders ipso facto the intuitionist arguments, shaped to meet the positivist challenge, obsolete. Weber does not concede that lawmaking is the exclusive advantage of nomological disciplines, nor does he take pride in the fact that "human freedom" defies regulation as a matter of principle. Weber maintains that cultural phenomena are even more susceptible to lawmaking and regulation than are the natural phenomena (Weber, *Knies*, p. 125). But such general laws, regardless of how "subjectively adequate" they might be (e.g., the laws of economic conduct), are of little value for the causal explanation of concrete action. With this conviction Weber

took it upon himself to determine the extent to which the "normative and de facto" elements influence the realm of economy (an
intention that is implied in the original title of his *Economy and
Society*), rather than trying to further refine the abstract "laws of
man's economic behavior." Weber even goes so far as to claim that
the discovery of natural laws is of sheer heuristic value for all
sciences alike; nomological or historical, natural or sociocultural
(Weber, *Roscher*, p. 63).

At this point, it would be appropriate to add a few words about
the way Weber conceived of the relationships between the two
realms of natural and cultural sciences. We know that Weber did
not think much of the positivist claims about the superiority of their
methods in the study of sociocultural phenomena; he doubted the
adequacy of their conception of the natural world, as well as the
mission they ascribed to the nomological disciplines in capturing its
essence in their abstract formula: "It is not the 'actual' interconnec-
tions of 'things' but the *conceptual* interconnection of *problems*
which define the scope of various sciences" (Weber, *Objectivity*,
p. 68).

We also have shown that Weber rejected the prevalent notions
held by the protagonists of the intuitionist school regarding the
fundamental chasm between the two types of sciences. He did not
attribute this difference to the antinomy of the subject matters of
human and exact sciences, i.e., the inanimate, determined world of
nature as opposed to the meaningful, volitional action of the
human being in society (Weber, *Knies*, p. 185). *For Weber, the
domains of cultural and natural sciences are neither identical nor
mutually exclusive.* He founded his methodology on the basic assumption that the natural world and the cultural world are in
hierarchical order and their relationship is one of "genus-species."
"Action" is not the logical opposite of "behavior," it is a specific
kind of behavior, loaded with meaning attributed to it by the actor;
the social action is a subclass of the action. Human subjectivity does
not radically oppose the empirical world; it just makes a part of the
latter more complex. It is possible (Weber, *Knies*, p. 140) and
sometimes necessary (Weber, *Economy I*, p. 18) to use the methods
of the empirical sciences in the cultural sciences to understand some
cultural phenomena (Weber, *Economy I*, p. 10) or even to "verify"
interpretive hypotheses about them (Weber, *Knies*, p. 160). When

and where this should be performed is to be determined by the empirical research (Weber, *Knies*, p. 140). On the other hand, the methods most suited for interpretive sociology (i.e., the teleological rationalistic method of interpretation) can be of great heuristic value for the natural sciences (e.g., the use of the functional purposive scheme in physiology) (Weber, *Economy I*, p. 15).

Yet there are methods molded exclusively for the study of the cultural phenomena. But the differences between these methods and those of the natural sciences do not originate in ontological dissimilarities of their subject matter, but in different interests they are responsive to (Weber, *Knies*, p. 184–185). Therefore, if one uses the methods of natural sciences, one can catch a glimpse of the social world—the view behaviorists get. This view is not necessarily wrong, but lacking. By looking at social phenomena in this light, one is likely to "miss out" on a substantial amount of information that is available in the realm of the sociocultural phenomena (Weber, *Biology*, p. 389). Weberian sociologists do not categorically reject the use of the methods of the exact sciences in the exploration of social phenomena. Rather, they go beyond the discovery of correlations and functional relationships: they can accomplish something which is never attainable in the natural sciences, namely, the subjective understanding of the action of the component individuals. The natural sciences, on the other hand, cannot do this, being limited to the formulation of causal uniformities in objects and events and the explanation of individual facts by applying them. We do not "understand" the behavior of cells but can only observe the relevant functional relationships and generalize on the basis of these observations. This additional achievement of explanation by interpretive understanding, as distinguished from external observation, is, of course, attained only at a price—the more hypothetical and fragmentary character of its results. Nevertheless, subjective understanding is the specific characteristic of sociological knowledge (Weber, *Economy I*, p. 15).

Appendix B

On Verification of the Ideal Types: Winch, Schutz, and Oakes

Preserving the meaning that the social actor attributes to his or her behavior as an integral part of the social sciences presents interpretive disciplines with a difficult choice. They seem to have to either neglect or to otherwise fill or bridge the gap that invariably emerges between the understanding of the social actor and that of the scientific observer. Weber considered the problem but put off a rigorous attempt to solve it. He dismissed as unconducive and naive the suggestion that an empathetic identification with the subject can be used to fill the gap between the intended and observed meanings. A close reading of Weber's theory of concept formation also reveals that he did not deem it necessary or scientifically sound to bridge that gap through verification of interpretive inferences. Instead he devised his interpretive methods so that verification of interpretive schemes in the sense of collating them with the actual existing meaning or other empirical data would not be necessary. As this has been sufficiently discussed throughout the text, in this appendix we shall concentrate on the suggestions of Guy Oakes and Peter Winch, who, presupposing the necessity of verifying the ideal types, have proceeded to appraise Max Weber's theory of ideal types. We shall then turn to Alfred Schutz's critique of Weber's methodology with regard to this problem. Weber's rejection of the empathetic school was spelled out clearly enough to prevent any serious commentator from ascribing to him such ideas. But as these examples indicate, a scholarly inclination persists to attribute to Weber a solution (to the problem of the rift between intended and interpreted meanings) that involves "verification" of ideal types. The proponents of the verification thesis treat the ideal types like the theories of natural sciences; that is, as general statements about a class of actually existing phenomena, to be further validated and verified. This procedure is to be carried out through exposing the ideal typical "hypothesis" to the empirical data. The implication, in keeping with the tradition of natural sciences, would be that a single diversion between facts and theory must (ideally) culminate in the devaluation of the theory. Of course, as we have already mentioned, an ideal type is not debunked if the empirical reality or the intentionality of the "native" does not conform to it. Quite the contrary, it is, insofar as such diversions exist, of course, within a reasonable range, that the ideal types are useful. It must be borne in mind that in dealing with ideal types, we do not ask "whether or not" they "subsume" the reality; rather "to what extent" the reality "approximates" the ideal types.

Unlike Weber, Oakes's interest is a linguistic and logical one; it is not sociological. He is concerned about matters such as the truth conditions for the ascription of the constitutive concepts (Oakes, 1977, p. 23). In his introduction to Weber's *Roscher and Knies*, Oakes claims that the production of meaningful interpretations must be done "in such a way that it can be verified." However, the passage quoted from Weber in the footnote does not in any way support the idea suggested by Oakes. We have already made it clear that certain kinds of "meaning" need verification, but this does not apply to the ideal typical meaning constructions. Weber believed that "our habitual modes of thought and feeling" vouch the subjective adequacy of an interpretation. Even the determination of the "causal adequacy" of an ideal typical construct would not further or fortify the universality of its subjective adequacy. To gauge the causal adequacy of an ideal type is to demonstrate the extent to which the ideal type can be "useful" by showing the extent to which the reality deviates from it. The determination of the causal adequacy of an ideal type, therefore, is not an instrument of testing the "truth condition" of "social hypotheses" (Weber, *Economy I*, pp. 11–12). Guy Oakes, however, in his effort to bridge the hiatus that separates the social actor from the scientific observer, suggests that the scientific interpretation of the ideal type must be corroborated by the social actor's understanding. For this to happen, first the subjectivity of the social actor must be "reproduced." Only if the reproduced meaning is shown to be an exact replication of the ideal type can the ideal type satisfy Oakes's "*verstehen* criterion" and be finally accepted:

> If the investigation is successful, there is a sense in which it should mirror or reproduce the native's own account: the criteria which the social scientist employs for the ascription of a given [social] predicate should be equivalent to the criteria which the native employs for the ascription of the same (social) predicate. (Oakes, 1977, pp. 24–25)[1]

This verification involves two methodologically dangerous steps. First, the "reproduction" of the subjectivity of the native. We have already demonstrated how Weber went to great lengths to prove that this is an impossible and unnecessary task to undertake. Second, and by far the more dangerous step, consists of the matching of the ideal typical construction against the reproduced "actual existing meaning" or the "native's account." This latter step involves a reduction of the pure types to the actual existing meaning and, thus, removes the keystone of Weber's methodology and reverses its telos. It appears not to have occurred to Oakes that "the native's account" cannot be the ultimate criterion for the validity of the ideal types, simply because Weber introduced the possibility of "semiconsciousness" as well as "false consciousness" of the concrete social actor.

The same concern for verifiability of ideal types underlies Peter Winch's critique of Weber. In his *The Idea of a Social Science*, Winch criticizes Weber for suggesting that statistical correlations can be used to "verify" interpretations (Winch, 1977, p. 112). He also criticizes Weber for his "implied suggestion": "*Verstehen* is something which is logically incomplete and needs supplementing by a different method altogether namely, the collection of statistics." Then he goes on to criticize this allegedly Weberian viewpoint. His criticism is valid, but it rejects only Winch's "idea" of Weber's methodology. Winch proposes, "The compatibility of an interpretation with the statistics does not prove its validity" (Winch, 1977, p. 113). This obviously is not contrary to Weber's position. Such concurrence would only prove that the ideal type in question is useful (not valid). Winch also seems to have confused the determination of "causal adequacy" of an ideal typical construction with the process of verification of general laws in the natural sciences.

Finally a reference must be made to Alfred Schutz, who criticized Weber for his perfunctory treatment of the varieties of subjective experience and especially for neglecting to deal with the disjunction that exists between personally experienced and the observationally or motivationally interpreted types of meaning (Schutz, 1967, pp. 7, 8). He expressly wished to clarify and radically analyze the tacit presuppositions of Weber's interpretive sociology. On the question of verifiability of ideal types, he seems to have accomplished this task. Schutz argues that actual existing meaning, and ideal typical meaning are fundamentally different[2] and that mutual understanding, even in everyday life, is problematic. Above all, he maintains that achieving total symmetry between the intended and interpreted meanings is impossible.[3] But this does not render interpersonal or sociological understanding unattainable,[4] as the rift between the two types of meaning is guaranteed to remain negligible. This is vouched for by the fact that the parties to any interaction share with each other and the observer a common objective context of meaning. This makes observational and motivational understanding possible and allows for the construction of the subjectively adequate ideal types. Together with Weber, Schutz maintains that verification of ideal types is not only impossible but also unnecessary.

In social sciences the mode of understanding is always the indirect observation of the world of predecessors or that of contemporaries.[5] Thus entering into a face-to-face relationship even for the purpose of checking the validity of the ideal type would ipso facto spoil the scientificity of the procedure.[6]

Besides, ideal types are by definition unverifiable.[7] They never refer to nor can they even be corroborated by individuals.[8] Schutz could, of course, have added to this list by mentioning that for Weber even the availability of a thorough motivational understanding of the concrete social actor does not alter the situation. For even if such an inner understanding comes into conflict with the ideal type, it does not necessarily refute the ideal type in question: "The 'conscious motives' may well even to the actor himself, conceal the various 'motives' and 'repressions' which constitute the real driving force of his action" (Weber, *Economy I*, pp. 9–10).

Appendix C

Weber and Islam

Weber's own generalizing observations about the religious needs of warriors, as reflected in religions that are tailored to these needs, tend to exclude Islam as one such religion. First, Islam's radical monotheism (singularity of the divine in principle) would thwart the warrior's characteristic penchant for polytheism, monolatry or henotheism (Weber, *Judaism*, p. 133). Second, belief in predestination and divine determination instead of irrational fate or "kismet," which was generally favored by the warriors, prevailed in the Quran and pervaded the attitude of the prophet and his disciples (Weber, *Economy I*, p. 575). Furthermore, pride, a necessary component of martial spirit, is abhorred in Islam as inimical to the spirit of religion, which demands "total submission" to God (Weber, *Social*, p. 291). Islam not only encourages religious humility but also contains concepts such as sin and salvation, which, in Weber's view, are not supposed to be particularly pleasing to the dignified religiosity of the warriors. Finally, Islam is not an exclusively masculine religion; it does not offer hierarchical promotion to its believers nor does it emphasize discipline any more than other occidental religions do. The last three characteristics are, however, found in two other religions that Weber associated with warriors: Zen Buddhism in Japan (Weber, *India*, p. 279), and Mithraism in Rome (Weber, *Economy*, pp. 475–76). In the former case, the ascetic and contemplative exercises of the Zen monks seem to have appealed to the professional warriors and to their appreciation of discipline. Mithraism offered Roman centurions not only an exclusively masculine religion but also an essentially magical and sacramental distribution of grace and the possibility of hierarchical advancement in its mystery ceremonies. It should be borne in mind that in both cases we deal with radically transformed versions of religions that in their original form had not been warrior religions. This may dissuade one from dubbing them as warrior religions in the sense that Weber means it in the case of Islam. In response to the question why Weber designated Islam, which has been both in its original form and in its social character an occidental religion, as the quintessential warrior religion, the following explanation may be offered. Weber based his ideal type of Islam on prevailing European stereotypes, for he never got around to devoting as much time to Islam as he did to Judaism, post-Reformation Christianity, and the religions of India and China. This explanation endows less psychological significance to Weber's slips and errors of omission in studying Islam than do other scholars of this area, namely, Bryan S. Turner. However, this is not meant to reject, but rather to complement, Turner's particular explanation of Weber's treatment of Islam (Turner, 1974, p. 141, 176).

Appendix D

Ideologies and Counter-Ideologies of Intellectuals in Occidental East and West: An Ideal Typical Model

Auguste Comte preferred the sovereignty of the "savants" to that of the people; for him social evolution meant that scientific politics would have to replace the irrationality of democratic politics (Comte, 1969, p. 275). His version of social evolution was geared to reject the Spencerian interpretation of the historical progress that developed independent of human volition and was impervious to artificial prodding.

Lester Frank Ward, Comte's American disciple, called Spencerian sociology "a gospel of inaction" and "a wet blanket on the enthusiasm of all who would follow social science" (Ward, 1894, p. 618). Ward made explicit what remained implicit in Comte. Cosmic and organic evolution were different from social evolution in that, in the latter, conscious (telic) action became the very agent of social evolution (Ward, 1903, pp. 15–17); spontaneous evolution belonged to lower stages of evolution (Ward, 1844, p. 276). Ward's ideology of intellectuals' sovereignty, for which he coined the term "sociocracy," would not counter social evolution, but only terminate its spontaneous phase.[1] "Thus far social progress has in a certain awkward manner, taken care of itself, but in the near future it will have to be cared for" (Ward, 1926, p. 706). If we call arguments such as these the exceptionalist arguments, Ward could be said to have achieved the ultimate rationalization of it. Ward did not need to justify the intervention of humans in the process of evolution in the name of extraneous contingencies, because he argued that human "telic" intervention *is* the only form of social evolution in the modern age.

Having established the necessity of intervening in the process of social evolution, the ideologies of intellectuals must either establish or presuppose that their designated agents of intervention (savants, sociocrats as the vanguard of the proletarian party) will selflessly engage in their political task. They usually take the second path and simply share the platonic assumption that "a man who has learnt about right will be righteous" (Plato, *Gorgias*, Par. 460). Ward's sociocrats would be

> the last to claim an undue share. They work for all mankind and for all time, and all they ask is that all mankind shall forever benefit by their work. . . . They only ask an opportunity to apply scientific principles to great things. (Ward, 1926, p. 583)

Lenin claims the same purity for his leading elite, or, as he calls them, "a dozen tried and talented" (Lenin, 1973, p. 118). Although their title implies mere technical superiority, the leaders of the party were in fact entrusted with the grave task of shaping the consciousness of the proletariat, whom they were supposed to represent. The problem was that in Lenin's view the proletariat was prone to "opportunism" and was unable to transcend its economic concerns for ideal ones (Lenin, 1973, pp. 37, 69, 107).

The proponents of counterideologies of intellectuals in both traditions of sociology and socialism also seem to have used parallel tactics. Let us examine the positions of Rosa Luxemburg and William Graham Sumner in this category:

1. They uphold the sanctity of social evolution and object to human interventions in it. Their evolution makes no leaps. Sumner stated: "The only possible good for society must come of evolution not revolution" (Sumner, 1914, p. 207). Rosa Luxemburg likened evolution to a delicate developing organism whose natural pace must not be disturbed: "Stop the natural pulsation of a living organism, and you weaken it, and you diminish its resistance and combative spirit" (Luxemburg, 1970, p. 129). The interventionist cure of the proletarian consciousness for the party intellectuals attempted by Lenin, in her view, was worse than the disease itself:

"Historically, the errors committed by a truly revolutionary movement are infinitely more fruitful than the infallibility of the cleverest central committee" (Luxemburg, 1970, p. 130).

In short, the counterideologies of intellectuals upheld the full automaticity of social evolution. Even if history proceeds in a zigzag and prolonged fashion, they argued, it would be wiser to let it run its course than to unleash the "telic" or volunteeristic subjectivism of intellectuals in the hope of hastening or correcting it.

2. The counterideologies of intellectuals hesitate to waive the possibility of selfish manipulation of social change by the intellectuals who are supposed to shape it for the sake of universality. In the occidental West this suspicion takes the form of a simple mistrust of human nature. Sumner states: "The reason for excesses of the old governing classes lies in the vices and passions of human nature . . . these vices are confined to no nation" (Sumner, 1970, p. 27). In the occidental East, however, this argument is much more potent. Drawing upon the anarchist and Machdevist (derived from the name of the Polish-born Russian revolutionary Waclaw Machajski) traditions, the Eastern European counterelites have reduced Marxism and socialism to mere ideological facades for the rule of the intelligentsia. Of course, there is enough in Marx and Engels's compendium of writings to support the thesis of social determination of consciousness. It is on this very basis that Rosa Luxemburg chides Lenin for trusting the fate of the proletariat to "professional revolutionaries": "The 'intellectual' as a social element which has emerged out of the bourgeoisie and is therefore alien to the proletariat, enters the socialist movement not because of his natural class inclinations but in spite of them" (Luxemburg, 1970, p. 124).

The counterideologies of the Eastern European intellectuals state the case even more categorically:

> The intellectuals of every age have described themselves ideologically, in accordance with their particular interests, and if those interests have differed from age to age it has still been the common aspiration of the intellectuals of every age to represent their particular interests in each context as the general interests of mankind. The definition of universal, eternal, supreme (and hence immutable) knowledge displays a remarkable variability over the ages, but in every age the intellectuals define as such whatever knowledge best

serves the particular interests connected with their social role—and that is whatever portion of the knowledge of the age serves to maintain their monopoly of their role. (Konrad and Szelenyi, 1979, p. 14)

One can assume that they are inspired not only by Marx and Engels but by Bakunin and Machajski as well. The anti-intellectualism of anarchism had already denounced both Marxism and the elitism of utopian socialists. Bakunin held the reign of intellectuals to be "the most aristocratic, despotic, arrogant and elitist of all regimes" (Bakunin, 1972, p. 319). For him, the domination of the educated class over the uneducated would reproduce all their other differences, the demolition of which had been promised by the educated vanguards at the outset (Bakunin, 1953, pp. 77–81). Bakunin even foresaw the reign of bureaucratic intelligentsia as the final result of the elitism of intellectual ideology: the state, then, becomes the patrimony of a bureaucratic class (Bakunin, 1972, p. 96). Waclau Machajski turned Bakuninian anti-intellectualism into a universal conspiracy theory of intellectuals. He maintained, that the workers would not have their workers' government even after the capitalists have disappeared as the intelligentsia would continue to rule through the workers' deputies.

The structural similarities of ideologies and counterideologies of intellectuals in diverse traditions of socialism and sociology confirm the thesis that similar ideological needs can generate similar ideologies. Max Weber alluded to this possibility when he accounted for the development of similar ideologies of the welfare state in a variety of civilizational contexts (Weber, *China*, p. 143).

Appendix E

Epistemology and Methodology

Max Weber's theory of concept formation takes Rickert's and thus Kant's entire epistemology for granted. Therefore, Weber as a sociologist did not take it upon himself to enlarge on epistemological problems and neither should we. But a brief clarificatory note seems to be in order in view of recent critical comments that are directed at Weber's alleged epistemological confusion. These criticisms are the result of a conflation or collapsing of the epistemological and the methodological levels of concept formation. Kantian epistemology provides an answer to the problem of the incomprehensibility of reality, while neo-Kantian and especially Weberian methodologies deal with a world that is comprehensible yet infinitely rich. By ascribing a categorical form, such as existence, to the raw contents of our sensations, the Kantian epistemology turns the latter into "facts." An aggregate of these facts constitutes what Weber alternately calls "empirical" or "concrete" or "objective" reality. So when Weber claims that social sciences are the sciences of objective reality (*Wirklichkeitswissenschaft*), he is referring to an already categorically formed reality. According to Rickert the task of methodology is to reduce the infinite multiplicity of the empirical reality through methods of individualization (in historical or cultural sciences) and generalization (in exact sciences). To these methods of reduction Weber added the method of constructing ideal types. Therefore, it is an error to charge that Weber thought that ideal types must be compared with the prephenomenal reality in order to make the latter comprehensible (Oakes, 1987). Rather, the task of methodology is to discover methods by which a scientific reduction of a comprehensible yet infinitely complex reality can be

139

achieved (A. Sadri, 1987). Weber never implied that "the elements which are used to construct the concepts of both the natural and the social sciences are lifted directly from the 'infinite flux' of reality without conceptualization," as Hekman has charged. The Weberian remark to which this critique refers deals only with infinite multiplicity of empirical data not the "flux" of formless sensations (Hekman, 1983, p. 23). Later Hekman explicitly identifies the "infinite multiplicity" of reality, which is the condition of the empirical reality, with the "chaos" of reality, which apparently refers to the flux of the prephenomenal reality (Hekman, 1983, p. 30).

Weber believed that the generalizing methods of exact sciences as well as the individualizing and ideal type generating methods of social, historical, and cultural sciences all aim at achieving the same goal: reduction of the infinite multiplicity of empirical reality. It is the commonality of goal among the sciences, not the similarity of the methods of achieving it, that constitutes the basis of Weber's claim to scientific status of the social, historical, and cultural disciplines. In contrast to this view the mono-methodological approach of positivists sought to establish the scientificity of social sciences by conceding that the only possible manner of mastering the mass of empirical data is to follow the generalizing methods of the exact sciences which promised to banish the trivial and the unique while saving the "essential," that is the "general."

Unlike the proponents of "subjectivism" or "intuitionism," Weber did not link a critique of positivism to relinquishing all claims to the scientific status. Rather, he sought to legitimize the interest historians evince in the "unique" and the historically or culturally significant aspects of the world. While arguing for the applicability of the methods of exact sciences to the sphere of social, historical, and cultural sciences, Weber also maintained that the use of specific methods for achieving an interpretive understanding of the meaningful phenomena is indispensable for these sciences. Weber was able to uphold this complex position because he did not deem that the realm of meaningful phenomena excludes that of natural phenomena. Indeed, in one specific sense the realm of the social, cultural, and historical sciences is "the same" as the realm of nature: both can be reduced to and captured by generalizing methods of natural sciences. For Weber meaningful phenomena are at least as susceptible to generalization and prediction as are the natural phenomena. Weber conceived of the realm of meaningful phenomena not in opposition to but as a more complex region of the world of natural objects. His interpretive methods do not claim to be the only means of studying the realm of meaningful phenomena. Rather, they promise to provide a more sensitive and efficient set of apparatus for exploring and exploiting its complexities and possibilities. In other words, it is the difference of "interest" not the dissimilarity of the subject matter that necessitates the deployment of different methods for the study of natural and sociohistorical phenomena.

Notes

Chapter 1

1. An excellent exposition of this has been provided in the work of Thomas Burger, *Max Weber's Theory of Concept Formation.*

2. "Sciences are found and their methods are progressively developed only when *substantive* problems are discovered and solved. Purely epistemological or methodological reflections have never yet made a decisive contribution to this project. . . . Methodology can only be self-reflection on the means which have *proven* to be valuable in actual research. Explicit self-reflection of this sort is no more a condition for fruitful research than is knowledge of anatomy a condition for the ability to walk "correctly." In fact, whoever tried to walk by applying his knowledge of anatomy would be in danger of stumbling. The scholar who attempts to base the aims of his research on a foundation of extrinsic methodological considerations is in danger of falling into difficulties of the same sort" (Guy Oakes, Introduction to *Roscher and Knies*, pp. 14–15).

3. Quoted by Mommsen, "Max Weber's Political Sociology and his Philosophy of World History," p. 25.

4. Weber declares: "Action in the sense of subjectively understandable orientation of behavior exists only as the behavior of one or more individual human beings" (Weber, *Economy and Society*, vol. I, p. 13). In the case of other commonly used concepts, such as state, etc., Weber suggests that: "for the subjective interpretation of action in sociological work these *collectivities* must be treated as *solely the resultants and modes of organization of the particular acts of individual persons*, since these alone can be treated as agents in the course of subjectively understandable action" (Weber, *Economy I*, p. 13).

5. This was done in greater detail in *Critique of Stammler* (1971), a more refined version of which appears in the first chapter of his *Economy and Society*.

6. Max Weber, *Economy and Society*, first chapter.

7. In Weber's original text "*der tatsächlich . . . gemeinte sinn*" or actual existing meaning is opposed to "*[der] in einem begriffilch konstruierten reinen typus . . . subjektiv gemeinte Sinn*" or the subjective meaning of the theoretically conceived pure type.

8. This is evidence that Max Weber, following Rickert, presupposed a neo-Kantian epistemology according to which a flow of unformed sensations as is immediately present in human consciousness (let alone when reproduced in the mind of an observer) does not qualify as "knowledge" of concrete facts. Such sensations once categorically formed (e.g., as existing things, chronological successions, or as objectively possible trends, etc.) constitute the set of knowable facts. Once scientifically treated, i.e., selected through generalizing or individualizing methods of abstraction, these facts come to constitute the basis of concepts that are the building blocks of a scientific understanding. Without categories and without abstraction, it is impossible to talk of knowledge, let alone scientific knowledge. To "capture" the raw contents of the social actor's intentionality, therefore, would be a fruitless task. For a critique of more recent commentaries on the above controversy, see Appendix B. For an excellent elaboration of Weber's epistemology see Thomas Berger's *Max Weber's Theory of Concept Formation*.

9. By contrast, ideal types, as we will explain later, do not require "verification" in the sense in which hypotheses are verified in the natural sciences.

10. Alfred Schutz's efforts to unravel the constitution of the meaning for the solitary or interacting individual, are admittedly inconsequential for the social sciences, which are by definition interested in "indirect social observation" (Schultz, 1967, pp. 221, 223, 226, 229, 242). In turning away from the questions of concrete subjectivity of individuals, Weber seems to have anticipated Gadamer (*Truth and Method*, pp. 39, 166, 171, 236–240) and the later Wittgenstein (*Philosophical Investigations*, pp. 107, 116–132), who also chose to focus on the communal, intersubjective, and ultimately practical aspects of interpretation rather than refining and purifying the concrete subjectivity in isolation from its cultural and traditional surroundings.

11. "Meaning" may be of two kinds. The term may refer first to the actual existing meaning in the given concrete case of a particular actor, or to the average or approximate meaning attributable to a given plurality of actors; or secondly to the theoretically conceived *pure type* of subjective meaning attributed to the hypothetical actor or actors in a given type of action. (Weber, *Economy I*, p. 4)

12. See the quotation at the beginning of page 7.

13. First there is the "teleological," "rationalistic" reconstruction of the hypothetical course of human action. This is used in economic and socio-

logical theory. The historical individuals, condensed into concepts that single out and emphasize some of their significant aspects, constitute the second important variety of ideal types (historical ideal types). It is our contention (as in the case of the concept of rationality) that Weber was well aware of the differences in the different concepts he referred to by the same name. This is not a case of methodological confusion on Weber's part, but, at worst, a lack of clarification, due to carelessness, that has created so much controversy in the import of the concepts of ideal type or rationality. It must be of some value for those scholars who tend to overemphasize the distinction between historical and sociological ideal types to consider that for Weber these two occurred in the same genius. "Social action is for us the behavior of individuals, either historically observed or theoretically possible or probable, behavior related to the actual or anticipated potential behavior of other individuals" (Weber, *Logos*, p. 160).

14. See Appendix B for further discussion of this point.

15. Paul F. Lazarsfeld in his review of the voluminous results of social psychological surveys that were published under the title "The American Soldier, An Expository Review" demonstrates this with singular lucidity. He first tricks the reader into agreeing that a set of conclusions derived from the aforementioned surveys are self-evident and that their rediscovery would be a wasteful and futile practice. Then he reveals that the actual results were diametrically opposed to these ostensibly obvious statements, adding that these opposite conclusions would have also appeared "obvious" had they been stated first. He concludes, "Obviously something is wrong with the entire argument of 'obviousness.'"

16. Heidegger and Gadamer brought this aspect of Western social philosophy, which was only implicit in Weber, to full fruition.

17. Yet Weber argued for "ethical neutrality" in social sciences. This for him simply meant that the value judgments that in certain scientific projects turn up as the end result of an ostensibly objective research cannot possibly follow from the imputed scientific premises. Weber maintained that such valuations must appear autonomously, and not disguised as the final verdict of science—at the beginning rather than at the end of research. Values may then be put in suspended animation while the empirical investigation proceeds (Weber, *Meaning*).

18. In the rationalistic parlance of Descartes and Kant, "common sense" is close to or a synonym of "vulgar thinking." Vico, who has rightly been recognized as the first challenger of the Cartesian "monomethodological approach" to all sciences and the founding father of *verstehen* sociology, approached the question from a different angle. He appealed to common sense as a communally based judgment (Vico, *The New Science*, pp. 142, 350) whose goal was to reveal what is "important" and "right," not to seek

after the universally valid truth. Celebrating Vico's appreciation of common sense, Gadamer criticized Kant for once more relegating it to a purely subjective (and reflective) judgment of taste (Gadamer, pp. 19–39). Criteria for subjective adequacy of sociological ideal types evince a Vicoean appreciation for the common sense.

19. Habermas's critical remarks concerning the relativistic tendencies of Weber presuppose a more comprehensive and inclusive conception of social sciences and collapse the Weberian distinction between dogmatic and social sciences (Habermas, *Legitimation Crisis*, p. 110); 1979, pp. 178–185); 1981, The Theory, pp. 200–204). For a critical appraisal of Habermas in this connection see Hekman, 1983, pp. 138–145). Leo Strauss is also weary of the relativistic implications of Weber's thought (Strauss, 1953, pp. 45–70). Indeed, Weber would agree with his neo-pre-Aristotelian (Habermas, 1973, 41 ff.) and neo-Aristotelian critics that the social scientist can, is entitled to, and must pass value judgments on issues concerning his own as well as alien civilizations. He would, however, disagree that the social scientists in question must do so as a social scientist or in the name of science.

20. In Schutz's view only the study of the historical past poses the problem of lack of access to the "common core of knowledge" shared by the predecessors. By presupposing the homogeneity of the "contemporary civilization" for which he offers no justification, Schutz refuses to recognize the problem of cross-cultural interpretation. This neglect is evident in the following passage:

> My predecessor lived in an environment radically different not only from my own but from the environment which I ascribe to my contemporaries. When I apprehend a fellow man or a contemporary, I can always assume the presence of a common core of knowledge. The ideal types for the We- and They-relationships themselves presuppose this kernel of shared experience. That highly anonymous ideal type, "my contemporary," shares by definition with me in that equally anonymous ideal type, "contemporary civilization." Naturally this is lacking to my predecessor. The same experience would seem to him quite different in the context of the culture of his time. (Schutz, 1967, p. 210)

It is, of course, by no means self-evident that for the contemporary occidental the "common core of knowledge" shared by medieval European burgers would be more accessible than that shared by contemporary Indian yogis, Siberian shamans, or Japanese Zen masters.

21. Value-relevant interests are constitutive of both inter- and intracultural studies. Even within a culture the ideal types keep losing their illustrative functions owing to the ebbs and flows of historical interests. Therefore, the social sciences are condemned to "eternal youth" (Weber, *Objectivity*, p. 104).

22. Weber continues:

> This knowledge may function positively to supply an illustration, individualized and specific, in the formation of the concept of feudalism or negatively, to delimit certain concepts with which we operate in the study of European cultural history from the quite different cultural traits of the Incas and Aztecs; this latter function enables us to make a clearer genetic comparison of the historical uniqueness of European cultural development. (Weber, *Mayer*, p. 156)

23. Thomas Burger (p. 43) remains unimpressed with Rickert's solution concerning the inclusion of secondary data, that is, those facts that are apparently unrelated to the interest of the historian. Berger rightly observes that mere "tactfulness" and "taste" can hardly govern a scientific selection of the secondary facts. By broadening the concept of historical interest, Weber opened new avenues toward the resolution of this methodological problem.

24. "The type of social science in which we are interested is an *empirical science* of concrete reality (*Wirklichkeitswissenschaft*). Our aim is the understanding of the characteristic uniqueness of the reality in which we move" (Weberr, *Objectivity*, p. 72).

25. "[The use of historical ideal types] gives rise to no methodological doubts so long as we clearly keep in mind that ideal-typical developmental *constructs* and *history* are to be sharply distinguished from each other, and that the construct here is no more than the means for explicitly and validly imputing an historical event to its real causes while eliminating those which on the basis of our present knowledge seem impossible" (Weber, *Objectivity*, p. 102).

26. "Indeed, the partly brilliant attempts which have been made hitherto to interpret economic phenomena psychologically, show in any case that the procedure does not begin with the analysis of psychological qualities, moving then to the analysis of social institutions, but that, on the contrary, insight into the psychological preconditions and consequences of institutions presupposes a precise knowledge of the latter and the scientific analysis of their structure" (Weber, *Objectivity*, p. 88).

27. This does not exclude the use of ideal types for taxonomical and conceptual constitutive purposes in order to offer a preliminary definition of the object of investigation (Weber, *Stammler*, p. 123).

28. The ancient philosophical zeal for subsuming the particulars under the universal led to the ranking of analogical reasoning as inferior to inductive generalization and deductive inferences. The infatuation of Cartesian and positivist scientists with the discovery of eternal laws also led to a total depreciation of the analogical method. The champions of the methodological autonomy of human sciences, however, explored the un-

popular, nonorthodox logical and methodological avenues such as Vicoean "imaginative universals" (Vico, 1965), Weberian ideal types (Weber, *Protestant*, p. 47), and Wittgensteinean operationalism. The affinity of ideal types to analogies, therefore, is characteristic rather than unique. In other contexts Weber suggests a wider use of the historical comparative studies where study of analogous events takes precedence over isolating general aspects of the events in question (Weber, *Mayer*, p. 130).

29. Accepting unfalsifiable statements in scientific procedures appears to blur the Popperian demarcation line between science and metaphysics. However, in this we have only followed his own example. In his early deliberations on the philosophy of science, Karl Popper elaborated and consistently adhered to the principle of falsifiability as the only criterion for the distinguishing demarcation line of falsifiability. The twilight zone of "historical interpretation" thus allows for scientific unfalsifiability. Popper argues that to fight the extensive multiplicity of empirical reality the science of history must incorporate the value-relevant interest of the historian as a guide for selection and reduction of the data, or in his words: "Undoubtedly there can be no history without a point of view; like the natural sciences, history must be selective unless it is to be choked by a flood of poor and unrelated material" (Popper, 1961, p. 150). But, he goes on to explain, such selective approaches must not be mistaken for theories, a mistake he attributes to "historocists." The following is entirely compatible with Weber's view as represented in Chapter 1:

> As a rule these historical "approaches" or "points of view" *cannot be tested*. They cannot be refuted, and apparent confirmations are therefore of no value, even if they are as numerous as the stars in the sky. We shall call such a selective point of view or focus of historical interest, if it cannot be formulated as a testable hypothesis, a *historical interpretation*. (Popper, 1961, p. 151)

30. Considering all of these instances one wonders how Weber could be accused of not distinguishing between the meaning as experienced by the social actor, and that attributed to the social actors by the observer (Schutz, 1967, p. 8). The ideal type is clearly "ours," and we use it as a measuring device for gauging the uniqueness of the concrete reality.

31. Nonetheless, the proponents of Althuserian structuralism are horrified by Weber's introduction of cognitive interests into the objective process of causation: "Weber's metaphysical and fundamentally religious conception of the relation of man to the world of nature therefore entails a systematic epistemological relativism, a relativism defined at the level of cultural values rather than individual subjectivity, but a relativism nonetheless" (Hindess, 1977, p. 33). The structuralist critique of Weber's "episte-

mological relativism" is reminiscent of the neo-Aristotelian critique of Weber's "cultural relativism": they both shy away from defining the criteria for either cultural or epistemological universal and objective truth.

32. George Lukacs has consequently adopted Weber's category of objective possibility to demonstrate that the emergence of the proletarian class consciousness and ultimately socialist transformation is not an automatic or necessary development but an "objective possibility" (Lukacs, 1971, pp. 204–205; Arato, 1979, pp. 87–114).

33. In his critique of Edward Mayer, Weber used the interesting allegory of the throwing of regular as opposed to loaded dice to demonstrate the difference between "chance causation" and "adequate causation." Here the same example is further developed to virtually embrace all the concepts that have been discussed in this section. In regular dice, the chances of all six sides to come uppermost are equal. In this case we deal with "chance causality," the subject matter of calculus of probabilities. However, if the dice are "loaded," there is a favorable chance that a certain side will come out uppermost. Only here can we introduce the concept of "adequate causation" and the "objective probability" of the coming out of the side that is favored by the loading of the dice. Now to take Weber's analogy one step further, suppose a die is loaded so that it favors, by a chance of 99 to 1, the side that reads six. Also suppose that this die is tossed, but just before it stopped rolling an earthquake caused a slight jerk of the table. The determination of the causal significance of the earthquake depends on the outcome. If the outcome is still a six, then we shall argue that although the last movement was part of the causal chain that necessitated the final outcome, its causal effect can be treated as negligible. This is so because the coming uppermost of the number was "adequately caused:" the outcome was "objectively possible" from the beginning as it was favored by the process of loading. The final "accident," that is the movement caused by the earthquake, therefore, could, for all practical purposes, be replaced by any movement caused by other external factors, or it could even be altogether eliminated without any changes in the outcome. On the other hand, if in this case the side that reads any other number should come uppermost, we conclude that since the outcome was not favored by the objectively possible circumstances (i.e., the way in which the die was loaded) the final "accident" must be treated as causally important.

34. His two famous essays, "Social Psychology of the World Religions" and "The Religious Rejections of the World and Their Directions," clearly attest to this. Especially, see Weber, *Rejections*, p. 357; *Social*, p. 281.

35. This point will be discussed in detail in Chapter 3.

36. This point will be developed further in Chapter 2.

Chapter 2

1. In other words, Weber's sociology of religion and his sociology of intellectuals at once vindicated and transcended Marx's as well as most of the Marxist theories on the subject. However, it is feasible to envision Weber as a theorist who attempted to debunk Marxism, but this could be done only if the following conditions are satisfied: (a) It is maintained that Marx's sociology of religion is exhaustive, in which case amending it would be to challenge its comprehensiveness; (b) An attitude is adopted whereby one deductively attributes, and then reduces, all ideas to the constellation of interests, in which case the possibility of other modes of mutual influence and determination is excluded *a priori.*

2. This assertion, however, is followed by an explanatory note that sheds some light on the relationships between magic and prophecy. Weber was at pains to emphasize that prophets (especially emissary prophets) rejected the magical practices in favor of a complete rationalization of the religious sphere. The question might arise: How can there be so much hostility between magicians and prophets if one is the precursor of the other? Of course, the contrast is not so drastic because, despite their rejection of magic, the prophets sought to legitimize themselves to the masses through subtle claims to magical charisma. "With them, however, this has merely been a means of securing recognition and followers for the exemplary significance, the mission, or the savior quality of their personalities" (Weber, *Rejections*, p. 327).

3. These terms have been defined in Chapter 1.

4. It would be wrong to conclude that this discussion is an endorsement of Mannheim's concept of "free floating intellectuals." Mannheim takes the "possibility" of transcending class interests from Weber but transforms it into an exclusive privilege of the educated classes. Of course, the apparent naiveté of his theory is not the result of an "error" explicable in the framework of the "autonomous" sphere of academic contemplation. It is the direct effect of Mannheim's ideological zeal to which I have already alluded.

5. I do not wish to enter the discussion of rationality in this book, as Stephen Kalberg, Donald Levin, and Mahmoud Sadri seem to have discussed the matter sufficiently. See the bibliography for the relevant works of these authors.

6. All these assertions rest on Weber's basic ontological assumptions to which we shall return.

7. This point belongs in this section only if we concur that neither skepticism nor passionate denial of religion but only a categorical indifference toward it can be considered entirely irreligious.

8. It would, however, be one-sided to consider this statement in isolation from Weber's theory of ideas and interests because his theory is as inconducive to materialistic determinism as it is to any form of emanationism. "Intellectualism," Weber argued, "is only one source of religious ideas." Let us not forget that for Weber such intellectualism itself presupposes a set of material conditions, namely "leisure." He noted that "no new religion" has ever resulted from sheer contemplative religious search by intellectual circles "or from their chatter" (Weber, *Economy I*, p. 517; *India*, p. 236).

Chapter 3

1. See the vertical differentiation in the cross tabulation proposed in Chapter 4.

2. Hannah Arendt describes the predisposition of intellectuals who gravitated to fascism in the following passage: "They read not Darwin but the Marquis de Sade. If they believed at all in universal laws, they certainly did not particularly care to conform to them" (Arendt, 1968, p. 28). Leszek Kolakowski attempted to explain the popularity of radical antirationalism among modern intellectuals in terms of their collective psychology: "We may explain conversions of this type, in psychoanalytic terms, as a vengeance of id upon the excessively developed ego or, in social terms, as a result of the alienation that almost every intellectual experiences and that forces him to look for community other than the elitist *Republique des Lettres*, giving him the sense of confidence, spiritual security, and authority that is lacking in intellectual work" (Kolakowski, 1972, p. 11).

3. The similarity between this concept and that found among the Israelites is mostly apparent. Indeed, the absence of powerful kings and their state bureaucracy in ancient Israel might have precluded the notions of charity and the curse of the poor. But luckily for the poor, the Israelites shared the idea of collective punishment. If the cries of the poor were heard by Yahweh, the divine wrath would envelop not only the prince and his functionaries but also the whole nation.

4. The usage of this term is due to Professor Arthur Vidich.

Chapter 4

1. The word "intellectual" dates back to the Dreyfus affair in France. It was first used derisively but then embraced by the defenders of Dreyfus, including Zola and Durkheim. This word has retained the connotations of a high-minded and somewhat oppositional attitude that were implied in its

original usage. The word "intelligentsia," its Roman word cell notwith-standing, is of Russian or possibly Polish coinage. It referred to the vast numbers of the educated class that gradually appeared to distance them-selves from both the state bureaucracies and the nobility. Our usage is meant to capture some of the original flavor of opposition and high-mindedness in the case of "intellectuals" and the emphasis on the vast numbers and the importance of education in the case of "intelligentsia."

2. For a discussion of this topic see Appendix D.

Appendix A

1. Namely the post-Kantian German intuitionists.

2. As particular beings, we are "interested" in "our" past. It is a unique history that we seek to make sense out of. For occidentals of the late twentieth century, it is interesting to study the French Revolution and the two world wars (even when we study revolution or war in general), whereas, except in certain cases, we would not be interested in a particular natural object or process. For instance, we might study the general laws that govern the branching of the boughs of a certain species of tree, but we would scarcely be interested in the history behind the branching out of a particu-lar tree and the extent to which accidental happenings have interfered with the general law established for the species.

Our interest in our present is also directed by our situation as particular beings. The question of theodicy only among the intellectuals, and only in their intellectualizing moments, pertains to the meaning of the universe. Among the masses and other social strata and classes, however, the prob-lem of evil has always been relevant only insofar as the fate of particular individuals or groups of people are concerned.

The rootedness of this in the human condition is made obvious by E. E. Evans Pritchard who notes that witchcraft performs a similar function in the life of the Azande. Without neglecting the immediate causes of death or misfortune, the Azande tend to "explain" it by witchcraft. "In speaking to Azande about witchcraft and in observing their reactions to situations of misfortune it was obvious that they did not attempt to account for the existence of phenomena, or even the action of phenomena, by mystical causation alone. What they explained by witchcraft were the particular conditions in a chain of causation which related an individual to natural happenings in such a way that he sustained injury" (Pritchard, 1980, p. 21). Witchcraft for the Azande provides the missing link between the two appar-ently unrelated chains of causation that acted independently and coincided in such a way that brought misfortune upon a particular individual. "Witchcraft explains why events are harmful to man and not how they happen. Azande perceives how they happen just as we do" (Pritchard, 1980, p. 24).

Appendix B

1. Of course, knowing that Weber opposed this position in numerous passages of his methodological essays, Oakes qualifies this statement by the phrase: "There is a sense in which," and a footnote where he quotes Weber to the effect that this reproduction does not require any unanalyzable sympathetic feeling on behalf of the observer. Nor does it involve an "immediate" reproduction of the experience of the "native." But this still leaves us in the dark. We still do not know in "what sense" (and where) does Weber suggest that an ideal type must coincide with the "actual existing meaning" in the mind of the "native."

2. "There is a difference in kind between the type of naive understanding of other people we exercise in everyday life and the type of understanding we use in the social sciences. It is our task to find what distinguishes two sets of categories from each other: (1) those categories in terms of which the man in the natural standpoint understands the social world and which, in fact, are given to the social sciences as material with which to begin, and (2) those categories which the social sciences themselves use to classify this already performed material" (Schutz, 1967, p. 140).

3. "The postulate, therefore, that I can observe the subjective experience of another person precisely as he does is absurd. For it presupposes that I myself have lived through all the conscious states and intentional Acts wherein this experience has been constituted" (Schutz, 1967, p. 99).

4. "It might seem that these conclusions would lead to the denial of the possibility of an interpretive sociology and even more to the denial that one can ever understand another person's experience. But this is by no means the case. We are asserting neither that your lived experiences remain in principle inaccessible to me nor that they are meaningless to me. Rather, the point is that the meaning I give to your experiences cannot be precisely the same as the meaning you give to them when you proceed to interpret them" (Schutz, 1967, p. 99).

5. What, then, is the specific attitude of social science to its object, the social world? Fundamentally, it is the same as the attitude of the indirect social observer toward his contemporaries (Schutz, 1967, p. 99).

6. "This very 'possibility of being questioned' (*Befragbarkeit*) is a specific characteristic of the object of direct social observation" (Schutz, 1967, p. 156).

7. "Here there is no distinction between the meaning-context of the observer and that of the actor. The reason is simple: if there is a real person

corresponding to the observer's postulated ideal type, then he will by definition intend what the observer has in mind. However—and this is the basic postulate of social *science*—the motives ascribed to the ideal type must be both causally adequate and adequate on the level of meaning" (Schutz, 1967, p. 229).

8. No matter how many people are subsumed under the ideal type, it corresponds to no one in particular. It is just this fact that justified Weber in calling it "ideal."

Appendix D

1. The socialist ideologies of intellectuals have rarely enunciated their legitimizing claims with similar clarity. The exception to this rule is Lukacs's declaration that

> the blind power of the forces at work will only advance "automatically" to their goal of self-annihilation as long as that goal is not within reach . . . the blind forces really will hurtle blindly towards the abyss, and only the conscious will of the proletariat will be able to save mankind from impending catastrophe. (Lukacs, 1971, p. 70)

Bibliography

Arato, Andrew. *The Young Lukacs and the Origins of Western Marxism.* New York: Seabury Press, 1979.

Arendt, Hannah. *Totalitarianism.* New York: Harcourt, Brace and World Inc., 1968.

Aristotle. *The Nicomachean Ethics.* Translated by J. A. K. Thompson. New York: Penguin Press, 1979.

Aristotle. *The Politics.* Translated by T. A. Sinclair. New York: Penguin Books.

Aron, Raymond. "The Logic of the Social Sciences." In *Max Weber*, edited by Dennis Wrong. Englewood Cliffs, NJ: Princeton University Press, 1970.

Aron, Raymond. *Opium of Intellectuals.* Translated by Terance Marting. New York: W. W. Horton & Co., 1962.

Bakunin, Michael. "The International and Karl Marx." In *Bakunin and Anarchy*, edited by Dolgoff. New York: Vintage Books, 1972.

Bakunin, Michael. "Science and Authority." In *The Political Philosophy of Bakunin*, edited by G. P. Maximoff. London: Free Press of Glencoe, No. 4, 1953.

Beetham, David. *Max Weber and the Theory of Modern Politics.* Cambridge: Polity Press, 1985.

Bender, Thomas. *New York Intellect.* Baltimore: Johns Hopkins University Press, 1987.

Bendix, Reinhard. *Max Weber, An Intellectual Portrait.* Berkeley: University of California Press, 1977.

Burger, Thomas. *Max Weber's Theory of Concept Formation: History, Laws and Ideal Types.* Durham: Duke University Press, 1987.

Bernard, Thomas. *The Consensus-Conflict Debate.* New York: Columbia University Press, 1983.

Birnbaum, Norman. "Conflicting Interpretation of the Rise of Capitalism: Marx and Weber." *British Journal of Sociology*, 1953.

Bloch, Ernst. *Man on His Own*. New York: Herder and Herder, 1970.

Bloch, Ernst. *On Karl Marx*. New York: Herder and Herder, 1971.

Bloom, Allan. Interpretive essay. In *The Republic of Plato*. Translated by Allan Bloom. New York: Basic Books, 1968.

Cohen, Jere, Hazelrigg, Lawrence E., Pope, Whitney. "DeParsonizing Weber, A Critique of Parsons' Interpretation of Weber's Sociology." *American Sociological Review* 40 (1975): 229–241.

Comte, Auguste. "Plan on the Scientific Orientation Necessary for Reorganizing Societies." In *On Intellectuals*, edited by Philip Rieff. Garden City: Doubleday, 1969, pp. 248–283.

Coser, Lewis A. *Continuities in the Study of Social Conflict*. New York: Free Press, 1967.

Coser, Lewis A. *The Functions of Social Conflict*. New York: Free Press, 1956.

Coser, Lewis A. *Men Of Ideas*. New York: Free Press, 1965.

Dahlmann, Dittmar. "Max Weber's Relation to Anarchism and Anarchists: The Case of Ernst Toller. In *Max Weber and His Contemporaries*, edited by Wolfgang Mommsen and Jürgen Osterhamm. London: German Historical Institute, 1987.

Dahrendorf, Ralf. *Class and Class Conflict in Industrial Society*. Stanford: Stanford University Press, 1957.

Dahrendorf, Ralf. "Toward a Theory of Social Conflict." *Journal of Conflict Resolution* 11: 170–183.

Dahrendorf, Ralf. "The Social Function of the 'Fool' in the Twentieth Century." In *On Intellectuals*, edited by Philip Rieff. Garden City: Doubleday, 1969, pp. 49–53.

De Hausar, George, B., ed. *The Intellectuals: A Controversial Portrait*. Glencoe: Free Press, 1960.

Dijlas, Milovan. *The New Class, An Analysis of the Communist System*. New York: Fredrich A. Praeger Publishers, 1957.

Gadamer, Hans Georg. *Truth and Method*. New York: Seabury Press, 1975.

Gouldner, Alvin. *The Future of Intellectuals and the Rise of the New Class*. New York: Seabury Press, 1979.

Gramsci, Antonio. "Intellectuals." In *Prison Notebooks*, edited by Quintin Hoare and Geoffrey Nowell Smith. New York: International Publishers, 1978.

Habermas, Jurgen. *Communication and the Evolution of Society*. Translated by Thomas McCarty. Boston: Beacon Press, 1979.

Habermas, Jurgen. *Legitimation Crisis*. Translated by Thomas McCarty. Boston: Beacon Press, 1975.

Habermas, Jurgen. *The Theory of Communicative Action*, Vol. I. Translated by Thomas McCarty. Boston: Beacon Press, 1981.

Habermas, Jurgen. *Theory and Practice*. Translated by John Viertel. Boston: Beacon Press, 1973.

Hekman, Susan. *Weber, The Ideal Type and Contemporary Social Theory*. Notre Dame: University of Notre Dame Press, 1983.

Hindess, Barry. *Philosophy and Methodology in The Social Sciences*. Atlantic Highlands, NJ: Humanities Press, 1977.

Hofstadter, Richard. *Anti-Intellectualism In American Life*. New York: Vintage Books, 1962.

Honigsheim, Paul. *On Max Weber*. New York: Free Press, 1968.

Jacoby, Russel. *The Last Intellectuals*. New York: Noonday Press, 1987.

Kalberg, Stephan. "Max Weber's Types of Rationality: Cornerstones for the Analysis of Rationalization Process in History." *American Journal of Sociology*, Vol. 85, No. 5.

Kolakowski, Leszek. "Intellectuals Against Intellect." *Daedalus*, Summer 1972.

Kolakowski, Leszek. *Toward a Marxist Humanism*. New York: Grove, 1968.

Konrad, George, and Szelenyi, Ivan. *Intellectuals on the Road to Class Power*. Translated by Andrew Arato and Richard E. Alen. New York: Helen and Kurt Wolff, 1979.

Lazarsfeld, Paul F. "The American Soldier, An Expository Review." *The Public Opinion Quarterly* 13, 3 (Fall, 1979).

Lederer, Emil. *State of the Masses*. New York: W. W. Norton and Company, 1940.

Lenin, V. I. *Religion*. New York: International Publishers, 1935.

Lenin, V. I. *What is to be Done?* Moscow: Progress, 1973.

Levine, Donald N. *The Flight from Ambiguity, Essays in Social and Cultural Theory*. Chicago: Chicago University Press, 1985.

Lukacs, George. *History and Class Consciousness*. Translated by Rodny Livingstone. Cambridge: MIT Press, 1971.

Luxemburg, Rosa. "Organizational Question of Social Democracy." In *Rosa Luxemburg Speaks*, edited by Mary Alice Waters. New York: Pathfinder, 1970.

Macpherson, C. B. *The Life and Times of Liberal Democracy*. New York: Oxford University Press, 1977.

Madison, James, Hamilton, Alexander, and Jay, John. *The Federalist Papers*, edited by Clinton Rossita. New York: New American Libraries, 1961.

Mannheim, Karl. *Diagnosis of our Time: Wartime Essays of a Sociologist*. London: Routledge & Kegan Paul, 1943.

Mannheim, Karl. *Ideology and Utopia: An Introduction to Sociology of Knowledge*. New York: Harcourt, Brace and Company, 1936.

Marx, Karl. "Toward the Critique of Hegel's Philosophy of Law: Introduction." In *Writings of the Young Marx on Philosophy and Society*. Garden City: Doubleday, Anchor, 1967.

Mill, John Stuart. *On Liberty*. New York: Penguin, 1986.

Mommsen, Wolfgang. "Max Weber's Political Sociology and his Philosophy of World History." *International Social Science Journal* 17 (1965).

Oakes, Guy. Introduction to *Roscher and Knies: The Logical Problems of Historical Economics*, by Max Weber. New York: Free Press, 1975.

Oakes, Guy. Introduction to *Critique of Stammler*, by Max Weber. New York: Free Press, 1977.

Oakes, Guy. "Max Weber and the Southwest German School: Remarks on the Genesis of the Concept of the Historical Individual." *International Journal of Politics, Culture and Society* 1, 1, (1987).

Orwell, George. "Writers and Leviathan." In *The Intellectuals*, edited by George B. De Hausar. Glencoe: Free Press, 1960, pp. 270–271.

Poggioli, Renato. *The Theory of the Avant-Garde*. Cambridge: Harvard University Press, 1968.

Parsons, Talcott. Introduction to *The Theory of Social and Economic Organization*, by Max Weber. Translated by Talcott Parsons. New York: Free Press, 1964.

Parsons, Talcott. "The Intellectual: A Social Role Category." In *On Intellectuals*, edited by Philip Rieff. Garden City: Doubleday, 1969, pp. 3–25.

Plato. *Gorgias*. Translated by Walter Hamilton. New York: Penguin Books, 1971.

Plato. *The Republic of Plato*. Translated by Allan Bloom. New York: Basic Books, 1968.

Plato. *Statesman*. Translated by J. B. Skemp. New York: Bobbs-Merrill, 1957.

Popper, Karl. *The Logic of Scientific Discovery*. New York: Harper Torchbooks, 1968.

Popper, Karl. *The Poverty of Historicism*. New York: Harper & Row, 1961.

Popper, Karl. *The Open Society and Its Enemies, Vol. 1, The Spell of Plato*. Princeton: Princeton University Press, 1971.

Popper, Karl. *The Poverty of Historicism*. New York: Harper Torchbooks, 1961.

Pritchard, E. E. Evans. *Witchcraft, Oracles, and Magic Among the Azande*, edited by Eva Gillies. New York: Oxford University Press, 1980.

Rieff, Philip. *On Intellectuals*. Garden City: Doubleday, 1969.

Ritzer, George. *Sociology of Multiple Paradigm Science*. Boston: Allyn and Bacon, 1975.

Sadri, Ahmad. "Max Weber and the Southwest German School: Remarks on the Genesis of the Concept of the Historical Individual." *International Journal of Politics, Culture and Society* 1, 1 (1987).

Sadri, Mahmoud. "Reconstruction of Max Weber's Notion of Rationality: An Immanent Model." *Social Research* 9, 3 (Autumn 1982): 616-633.

Schumpeter, Joseph. *Capitalism, Socialism and Democracy*. New York: Harper Colophon, 1975.

Shils, Edward. "Intellectuals." In *International Encyclopedia of the Social Sciences*, edited by David L. Sills, Vol. 7. New York: Macmillan and the Free Press, 1968.

Shils, Edward. "The Intellectuals and the Powers: Some Perspectives for Comparative Analysis." In *On Intellectuals*, edited by Philip Rieff. Garden City: Doubleday, 1969, pp. 25-49.

Strauss, Leo. *Natural Right and History*. Chicago: University of Chicago Press, 1953.

Stuart, Samuel. "English Intellectuals and Politics in the 1930s." In *On Intellectuals*, edited by Philip Rieff. Garden City: Doubleday, 1969, pp. 196-248.

Sumner, William Graham. "The New Social Issue." In *The Challenge of Facts and Other Essays*. New Haven: Yale University Press, 1914.

Sumner, William Graham. *What Social Classes Owe to Each Other*. New York: Harper and Brothers, 1920.

Tocqueville, Alexis de. *Democracy in America*. Translated by George Lawrence. Garden City: Anchor Books, Doubleday, 1969.

Turner, Bryan. *Weber and Islam*. London: Routledge & Kegan Paul, 1974.

Van Leeuwen, Arend. *Critique of Heaven*. New York: Scribner's Sons, 1972.

Vico, Giambattista. *The New Science*, edited by T. G. Berger and M. H. Fisch. Ithaca: Cornell University Press, 1965.

Wald, Alan M. *The New York Intellectuals*. Chapel Hill: University of North Carolina Press, 1987.

Ward, Lester Frank. *Dynamic Sociology*. New York: D. Appleton, 1926.

Ward, Lester Frank. *Outline of Sociology*. London: Macmillan, 1844.

Ward, Lester Frank. "Political Ethics of Herbert Spencer." *Annals of American Academy* 1894, IV: pp. 582-619.

Ward, Lester Frank. *Pure Sociology*. London: Macmillan, 1903.

Weber, Max. "Sociology and Biology." In *Max Weber, Selections in Translation*, edited by W. G. Runciman. New York: Cambridge University Press, 1980.

Weber, Max. "Bureaucracy." In *From Max Weber*, edited by H. H. Gerth and C. Wright Mills. New York: Oxford University Press, 1958.

Weber, Max. "The Sociology of Charismatic Authority." In *From Max Weber*, edited by H. H. Gerth and C. Wright Mills. New York: Oxford University Press, 1958.

Weber, Max. *Religion of China*, edited by H. H. Gerth. New York: Free Press, 1957.

Weber, Max. "Class, Status, Party." In *From Max Weber*, edited by H. H. Gerth and C. Wright Mills. New York: Oxford University Press, 1958.

Weber, Max. "The Meaning of Discipline." In *From Max Weber*, edited by H. H. Gerth and C. Wright Mills. New York: Oxford University Press, 1958.

Weber, Max. *Economy and Society*, vol. I, edited by G. Roth and C. Wittich. Berkeley: University of California Press, 1978.

Weber, Max. *Economy and Society*, vol. II, edited by G. Roth and C. Wittich. Berkeley: University of California Press, 1978.

Weber, Max. "Freedom of the Universities." In *Max Weber on Universities*, edited by Edward Shils. Chicago: University of Chicago Press, 1973.

Weber, Max. *General Economic History*. New Brunswick: Transaction Books, 1981.

Weber, Max. "Capitalism and Rural Society in Germany." In *From Max Weber*, edited by H. H. Gerth and C. Wright Mills. New York: Oxford University Press, 1958.

Weber, Max. *The Religion of India*, edited by H. H. Gerth and D. Martindale. New York: Free Press, 1958.

Weber, Max. *Ancient Judaism*, edited by H. H. Gerth and D. Martindale. New York: Free Press, 1952.

Weber, Max. "National Character and the Junkers." In *From Max Weber*, edited by H. H. Gerth and C. Wright Mills. New York: Oxford University Press, 1958.

Weber, Max. "Knies and the Problem of Irrationality." In *Roscher and Knies*. New York: Free Press, 1975.

Weber, Max. "Some Categories of Interpretive Sociology." *The Sociological Quarterly* 22 (Spring, 1981).

Weber, Max. "Critical Studies in the Logic of the Cultural Sciences: A Critique of Eduard Mayer's Methodological Views." In *The Methodology of Social Sciences*, edited by Edward A. Shils and Henry A. Finch. New York: Free Press, 1949.

Weber, Max. "The Meaning of Ethical Neutrality." In *The Methodology of Social Sciences*, edited by Edward A. Shils and Henry A. Finch. New York: Free Press, 1949.

Weber, Max. "Objectivity in Social Sciences and Social Policy." In *The*

Methodology of Social Sciences, edited by Edward A. Shils and Henry A. Finch. New York: Free Press, 1949.

Weber, Max. "Politics as a Vocation." In *From Max Weber*, edited by H. H. Gerth and C. Wright Mills. New York: Oxford University Press, 1958.

Weber, Max. "Economic Policy and the National Interest in Imperial Germany." In *Selections in Translation*, edited by W. G. Runciman. New York: Cambridge University Press, 1980.

Weber, Max. *The Protestant Ethic and the Spirit of Capitalism*. New York: Charles Scribner's Sons, 1930.

Weber, Max. "Religious Rejections of the World and Their Directions." In *From Max Weber*, edited by H. H. Gerth and C. Wright Mills. New York: Oxford University Press, 1958.

Weber, Max. "Roscher's Historical Method." In *Roscher and Knies*. New York: Free Press, 1975.

Weber, Max. "Prospects for Democracy in Tsarist Russia." In *Max Weber, Selections in Translation*, edited by W. G. Runciman. New York: Cambridge University Press, 1980.

Weber, Max. "Science as a Vocation." In *From Max Weber*, edited by H. H. Gerth and C. Wright Mills. New York: Oxford University Press, 1958.

Weber, Max. "The Protestant Sects and the Spirit of Capitalism." In *From Max Weber*, edited by H. H. Gerth and C. Wright Mills. New York: Oxford University Press, 1958.

Weber, Max. "The Social Psychology of the World Religions." In *From Max Weber*, edited by H. H. Gerth and C. Wright Mills. New York: Oxford University Press, 1958.

Weber, Max. "Socialism." In *Max Weber: The Interpretation of Social Reality*, edited by J. E. T. Eldridge, New York: Schocken Books, 1971.

Weber, Max. *Critique of Stammler*. New York: Free Press, 1977.

Winch, Peter. *The Idea of a Social Science*. Atlantic Highlands, NJ: Humanities Press, 1977.

Wittgenstein, Ludwig. *Philosophical Investigations*. Translated by G. E. M. Anscombe. New York: Macmillan Publishing Co., 1958.

Znaniecki, Florian. *The Social Role of the Man Of Knowledge*. New York: Octagon Books, 1965.

Index